LOcaL

Culture

FAMILY ROOM
EDITION

For information about school-wide professional development, team training, or indi-vidual coaching in the application of Loving our Students on Purpose, please contact:

- www.godwinconsulting.com.au
- admin@godwinconsulting.com.au

Editor: Allison Slack
Cover Design by Ashley Beck
Interior Design and Layout by Daniel Morales
ISBN: 978-0-6459046-9-7

DEDICATION

This book is dedicated to Torrens Valley Christian School, who are courageously leading their school families on the journey of Loving Our Students on Purpose. Your example is paving the way for other communities to engage families and build cultures of connection, joy, and responsibility.

Books

Loving our Students on Purpose
Cultural Architect (coming 2026)

LoSoP Momentum Series

(Weekly aligned foundational philosophy of Loving our Students on Purpose)
Staffroom Edition––book, ebook, or video series available
Future editions coming soon!

LoSoP Culture Series

(Weekly aligned foundational values to build a Culture of Love)
Boardroom Edition
Staffroom Edition
Primary Classroom Edition
Secondary Classroom Edition
Family Room Edition

Podcasts

Loving Our Students on Purpose Journey Podcast
Culture Daily: Education Edition

Resources Available

www.godwinconsulting.com.au
Explore our full range of LoSoP resources designed to bring connection and joyful responsibility into everyday practice—from Desk Flips, Printable Poster Collections, and Flash Cards to Online Courses, Bookmarks, and more.

For bulk purchases email admin@godwinconsulting.com.au

TABLE OF CONTENTS

BUILDING A CULTURE OF LOVE

Welcome to the LoSoP Culture Series: Family Room Edition

*Creating a Home Where Every Person Feels Beloved,
Chosen, and Cherished*

This series is your invitation to create something lasting: a culture of love in your home where every person feels beloved, chosen, and cherished. Whether your family is big or small, loud or quiet, or in a season of calm or chaos, this series will help you grow closer together, build trust, and become a family where love leads the way.

The *LoSoP Culture Series* is built on a simple but powerful truth: love changes everything—not the soft or sentimental kind of love, but the kind that shows up with boundaries, grace, and purpose. The kind of love that tells the truth, makes space for differences, and gently repairs what fear or frustration might have broken.

Over 40 weekly sessions, your family will explore the key ingredients that build strong relationships and connected culture at home. Each week focuses on one principle of connection, drawn from four foundational pillars: *Healthy Relationships, Joyful Responsibility, Genuine Restoration,* and *Leadership Development.*

This series is part of a broader movement happening across schools, staffrooms, workplaces, and boardrooms—where families, educators, and leaders are learning the same core ideas, at the same time, in their own spaces. So if you're connected to a school or workplace also using this series, you'll be sharing language, values, and moments of growth together.

What Is a Culture of Love?

A culture of love doesn't happen by accident—it's built on purpose. It's made in the small choices we make every day: to speak kindly, to repair when we've hurt each other, to hold one another accountable with grace, and to lead our family in a way that nurtures connection instead of control.

This series is guided by four big ideas:

1. Our goal is connection.
2. Love is a powerful choice.
3. Fear is the enemy of connection.
4. Building and protecting connection is a learning journey.

Each week, you'll come back to these truths as you learn, share, and grow together.

The Four Pillars of a Family Culture of Love

As a family, you'll explore one or more of these four pillars each week:

- Healthy Relationships––where every voice matters and everyone feels safe

- Joyful Responsibility--where each person owns their choices and contributes to the family
- Genuine Restoration--where mistakes are repaired and connection is restored
- Leadership Development--where kids and adults alike learn to lead with empathy and courage

These pillars will help your family become stronger, kinder, and more connected—even on the tough days.

How to Use This Series

Each session is designed to be simple and flexible. You can gather around the dinner table, on the couch, or even in the car. Each week includes a keyword, a family phrase, space to create your own definition, real-life reflections, questions to chat about, and an idea to practise during the week.

You don't have to get it right every time—just keep showing up for each other.

Why It Matters

In the rush of daily life, it's easy to lose sight of the kind of family you want to become. This series helps you slow down, connect meaningfully, and be intentional about what matters most. Together, you'll shape a family culture where every person is seen, heard, and loved—and where connection grows stronger, one week at a time.

This is a home built on love—on purpose.

A NOTE FROM BERNII

Dear Families,

Welcome to the *LoSoP Culture Series: Family Room Edition*—a resource created to support you in building the kind of home where love leads, mistakes are met with grace, and every person feels they truly belong.

As a parent myself, I know how busy and stretched family life can feel. Between meals, mess, emotions, routines, and everything else, it can be easy to lose sight of what kind of culture we're actually creating at home. This series is here to help you slow down—just once a week—and be intentional about the kind of family you're becoming.

Each week gives you space to talk about something that really matters: connection, responsibility, restoration, or leadership. You'll listen to one another, learn together, and practise small habits that strengthen the relationships in your home.

These aren't big, complicated lessons. They're simple, meaningful moments to help your children feel seen, heard, and valued—and to help you, as a parent, lead with courage and kindness, even on the hard days.

You don't have to get it all right. That's not what this is about. You just have to keep showing up with love, honesty, and a willingness to grow—together.

Thank you for being the kind of parent or caregiver who chooses presence over perfection, connection over control, and grace over guilt. Your home doesn't need to be perfect to be powerful—and every conversation you share this year is laying the foundation for something beautiful.

I'm cheering you on from my own family room to yours.

With love,
Bernii

HOW TO USE THIS SERIES
—FAMILY ROOM EDITION

Creating a Home Where Every Person Feels Beloved, Chosen, and Cherished

The *LoSoP Culture Series: Family Room Edition* is a practical and flexible resource designed to help families build deeper connection, grow in shared responsibility, and nurture a strong, loving culture at home.

Each week provides a simple, structured way to start meaningful conversations, practise life-giving habits, and develop a shared language of values together. This isn't about getting it right or being perfect—it's about creating small, intentional moments that shape who you are becoming as a family.

Aligned with the LoSoP Classroom Edition

If your school is using the *LoSoP Culture Series: Classroom Edition* (Primary or Secondary), this Family Room Edition follows the same weekly topics—helping your home and school culture grow together. It creates a powerful opportunity for children, teachers, and families to speak the same language of connection, responsibility, and love.

You'll also find 16 additional *Holiday Activities* that keep the learning going in fun, meaningful ways—even when school's out.

Weekly Sessions

Each 10-week block explores a key idea designed to help your family grow in four foundational areas:

- **Healthy Relationships**
- **Joyful Responsibility**
- **Genuine Restoration**
- **Leadership Development**

Every session follows a clear and consistent structure:

Family Phrase

Each session begins with an *In This Family* phrase—a short, powerful statement that captures the heart of the week. Repeat it often throughout the week and let it become part of your family's shared culture.

For example:

"In this family, we listen with our hearts—because every voice matters."

Key Word & Definition Discussion Activity

You'll then introduce the week's Key Word. Instead of giving a set definition, invite every family member to share what the word means to them. This is called your *Definition Discussion*.

Ask: *"What do you think this word means?"*

At the end of the session, you'll write down your Family Definition together—creating a language that belongs to your family, not just the adults.

Learn

This section introduces the week's big idea in a simple, relatable way. Use your own examples or choose a story that helps your family connect with the concept.

Let's Make It Real

Here, you'll find a short metaphor, reflection, or story to bring the idea to life. Parents and carers are encouraged to role model vulnerability by going first—sharing a story from your own life. This helps create safety and shows children that growth is something we all practise, not just something they're expected to learn.

Discuss

Use the conversation questions to invite everyone into the discussion. Create space for each voice—especially those who are quieter or more reflective. Remind everyone of the importance of listening with their hearts, and bring back your Family Phrase if needed.

Adapt the questions to suit your family—feel free to add your own or skip those that don't fit.

Do

Each session includes a practical *Family Activity* to help bring the week's concept into real life. These are simple and adaptable for all ages—designed to fit into everyday family moments.

End-of-Week Reflection

At the end of the week, take time to reflect as a family:

- *How did we practise this idea?*
- *What moments stood out this week?*
- *What do we want to keep doing together?*

Finish by writing your Family Definition of the Key Word—adding it to your growing collection of shared language.

Why Define Key Words Together?

When families define key words together, they create shared understanding—and shared understanding builds culture.

Words like *respect*, *trust*, or *responsibility* might mean something different to each person. Taking time to ask, listen, and agree on what they mean in your family helps every voice feel heard and gives everyone ownership in building your values.

When children help define the words, they're more likely to remember them, live them, and take pride in the culture they helped create.

Flexible Timing

These sessions are designed to fit into everyday family life—during dinner, before bedtime, on the weekend, or even in the car.

Some weeks may spark deep conversation. Others may feel light and fun. Let your family's rhythm guide you.

Optional Holiday Activities

To support connection during school breaks or quieter seasons, this edition includes 16 *Holiday Activities* that continue the culture-building journey. These are grouped around the same four focus areas:

- Healthy Relationships
- Joyful Responsibility
- Genuine Restoration
- A Culture of Love

Use them to keep your family connected, playful, and intentional—no matter the season.

Final Thoughts

The *LoSoP Culture Series: Family Room Edition* is more than a set of lessons—it's an invitation to build a home where love leads, connection is protected, and every person feels safe to grow.

Small moments create lasting impact.

By setting aside time each week to reflect, talk, and practise these values together, you are shaping a family culture that will influence your children—and generations to come.

Thank you for choosing to build this kind of home. Your family culture is your legacy—and you are creating it on purpose.

SETTING UP YOUR FAMILY CULTURE SPACE

A Visible Space for Connection, Growth, and Memories

As you journey through the *LoSoP Momentum: Family Room Edition*, we encourage you to create a *Family Culture Space*—somewhere in your home where you can collect memories, ideas, reflections, and reminders of what you're building together.

This could be:

- A blank wall in your living area
- A pin board in the kitchen
- The fridge door
- A large scrapbook or family journal
- A photo wall or collage
- A cork board, whiteboard, or noticeboard
- Or even a simple space on a shelf with a special notebook

This space is not about being fancy or perfect—it's about being visible and intentional.

What Can You Add to Your Family Culture Space?

Throughout the year, you might like to add:

- Your *Family Phrases* from each week
- Your *Family Definitions* of the key words
- Photos of your weekly activities and successes
- Notes or drawings from your children
- Reflections or stories from your End-of-Week discussions
- Favourite quotes or Bible verses
- Holiday Activity highlights
- Your final *Family Manifesto (see page 223 - 227)*

Why Create a Family Culture Space?

Having a visible reminder of your family's learning helps:

- Keep connection front and centre
- Celebrate progress and effort
- Show your children that what you're doing together matters
- Create a record of your family's journey that you can look back on with joy

This simple practice makes your values visible—and turns ordinary moments into lasting memories.

There's no right or wrong way to do it—make it your own and have fun adding to it over time.

This is your family's story in the making.

FAMILY CULTURE SPACE—ADD PHOTOS,
DRAWINGS, OR MEMORIES HERE

USE A FEELINGS WHEEL TO SUPPORT YOUR CONVERSATIONS

Before you begin the *LoSoP Culture Series: Family Room Edition* with your children, we recommend printing a large *Feelings Wheel* and displaying it somewhere visible in your home—like on the fridge, in the bathroom, or near where you'll have your family conversations.

You can find a variety of Feelings Wheels online by simply searching "Feelings Wheel." Choose one that suits the age and stage of your children.

While the weekly sessions may not always ask directly, *"How do you feel?"*—questions about feelings will naturally come up in your family discussions. Having a Feelings Wheel nearby is a great tool to support these conversations.

It can help children (and adults) move beyond basic words like sad, bad, mad, or glad—and encourage them to find a more specific emotion to describe what's going on inside.

This simple practice builds emotional vocabulary and helps children learn to express themselves with clarity, confidence, and responsibility—a key skill for connection, empathy, and self-awareness.

When asking about feelings, focus on supporting your child's own experience. Rather than asking, *"How did that make you feel?"* (which can unintentionally place responsibility outside of them), it's more helpful to ask: *"How do/did you feel?"*

This empowers children to take ownership of their emotional experiences—and helps them build the skills to regulate and express those feelings in a healthy way without externalising blame.

PART ONE

CULTIVATING HEALTHY RELATIONSHIPS AT HOME

In this section, families will learn how to build strong, meaningful connections with one another. Together, you will explore effective communication, the power of empathy, building trust, and genuine respect.

Rather than simply talking about relationships, families will actively practice these skills through engaging stories, meaningful conversations, and everyday scenarios. Healthy relationships don't just happen—they flourish when we intentionally choose kindness, active listening, and mutual care.

The goal is to help every family member feel confident in their ability to connect and to foster a home environment rich with respect, understanding, and compassion.

WEEK 1:

THE POWER OF LISTENING

"In this family, we listen with our hearts—because every voice matters."

Key Word: Listening

Start by asking everyone in the family:

"What do you think the word 'Listening' means?"

Take turns sharing your thoughts—there's no right or wrong answer.

We'll come back at the end to create our own *Family Definition* of Listening.

Learn

Listening is one of the most powerful ways we show love in a family. When we stop, look someone in the eye, and really pay attention, we tell them: *"You matter to me."*

Listening is more than staying quiet—it's about making space for someone else's words, ideas, and feelings.

At home, this might look like putting down devices, turning off the TV, not interrupting, and letting someone finish their story.

When we really listen to each other, we feel closer, safer, and more connected.

Consider

In a busy family, it's easy to talk *at* each other—giving instructions or rushing conversations.

But think about this:

Have you ever felt upset because no one was really listening to you?

Or have you ever felt really special because someone stopped and listened to you properly?

Listening makes love feel real.

Let's Make It Real

Let everyone have a turn sharing:

Tell us about a time when someone really listened to you. How did it feel?

Then share:

What do we find tricky about listening well in our family?

(E.g., interrupting, being distracted, jumping in with advice)

Discuss

Choose a few of these questions as a family:

- Why do you think listening is powerful in a family?
- What happens when people don't feel listened to?
- What could we do to become a better listening family this week?

Do

This week, practice *Family Listening Time*.

Choose one moment a day (maybe dinner time or before bed) where everyone listens while one family member shares something about their day—no interruptions.

Start simple. Maybe it's just: *"Tell us your high and low of the day."*

End-of-Week Reflection

Gather as a family and talk about:

- How did it feel to listen to each other this week?
- Did anyone notice it made a difference in how connected we felt?
- What will we keep doing to stay a "listening family"?

Family Definition

As a family, agree together:

What do we want the word 'Listening' to mean in our home?

Write your family definition here:

_____

_____

_____

_____

WEEK 2:

GIVING AND RECEIVING FEEDBACK WITH LOVE

*"In this family, we give and receive feedback with love
—because we care about our growth."*

Key Word: Feedback

Ask your family:

"What do you think the word 'Feedback' means?"

Talk about what comes to mind when you hear the word—and how feedback has felt in the past.

We'll come back at the end to create our own *Family Definition* of Feedback.

Learn

Feedback is when someone helps us grow by telling us what we're doing well and what we could do better.

Families that give and receive feedback with kindness create a safe place for everyone to learn and improve.

Giving feedback with love means:

- Speaking kindly
- Being helpful, not hurtful
- Saying it at the right time

Receiving feedback with love means:

- Listening without arguing
- Saying thank you
- Taking time to think about it

Consider

In family life, it's easy to point out what's wrong—but sometimes we forget to say what's going well.

But think about this:

Have you ever had someone tell you something in a helpful way that made you better?

Or has someone said something unkind that just made you feel bad, not better?

Feedback with love helps us grow—without hurting connection.

Let's Make It Real

Invite each person to share:

Tell us about a time when someone gave you feedback that really helped you.

Then share:

- What's tricky about giving feedback kindly in our family?
- What's tricky about receiving feedback well?

Discuss

Talk about these questions together:

- Why is feedback important in family life?
- How does feedback with love help us grow?
- What can we practise this week to give feedback kindly?
- How can we practise receiving feedback well?

Do

This week, practise giving feedback with love:

- Say something kind before giving advice.
- Ask first—"Would you like some feedback?"
- Say thank you when someone gives you feedback.

Look for moments to help each other grow in kindness and love.

End-of-Week Reflection

Gather as a family and talk about:

- Did anyone give or receive feedback with love this week?
- How did it feel to practise this in our family?
- What could we keep doing to make feedback feel safe and helpful in our home?

Family Definition

As a family, agree together:

What do we want the word 'Feedback' to mean in our home?

Write your family definition here:

_____

_____

_____

_____

WEEK 3:

GROWING EMPATHY IN YOUR FAMILY

"In this family, we care about how others feel—because love starts with understanding."

Key Word: Empathy

Ask your family:

"What do you think the word 'Empathy' means?"

Share ideas—when have you felt it or shown it?

We'll come back at the end to create our own *Family Definition* of Empathy.

Learn

Empathy means putting yourself in someone else's shoes. It's about imagining how they feel and caring about what they're going through.

Empathy makes our family stronger because it helps us:

- Understand each other better
- Be kind even when we disagree
- Support each other when things are hard

Empathy starts with asking:

"I wonder what that feels like for them?"

Consider

In family life, it's easy to focus on how *we* feel—but empathy helps us pause and think about others.

But think about this:

Have you ever had a hard day and just wanted someone to understand?

Or have you ever been surprised when someone showed you kindness even though they didn't know the whole story?

Empathy makes love feel safe and real.

Let's Make It Real

Go around the family and answer:

Tell us about a time when someone showed you empathy. How did it feel?

Then share:

Is it easier for us to show empathy in our family—or harder? Why do you think that is?

Discuss

Use these questions to guide your family conversation:

- Why is empathy important in family life?
- How do we know when someone needs empathy?
- What could we practise this week to grow our empathy at home?
- What would it look like to put yourself in someone else's shoes?

Do

This week, see what happens when you:

- Notice when someone looks upset or tired.
- Ask gentle questions like "Are you okay?" or "How can I help?"
- Take a moment to imagine what they might be feeling before you respond.

Look for chances to show kindness and care.

End-of-Week Reflection

Gather as a family and talk about:

- Did anyone show or receive empathy this week?
- How did it feel when someone stopped to understand how you were feeling?
- What could we keep doing to grow empathy in our family?

Family Definition

As a family, agree together:

What do we want the word 'Empathy' to mean in our home?

Write your family definition here:

_____

_____

_____

_____

WEEK 4:

COMMUNICATING WITH KINDNESS

"In this family, we speak love in a way others
can feel and understand."

Key Word: Kindness

Ask your family:

"What do you think the word 'Kindness' means?"

Share what kindness looks like, sounds like, and feels like.

We'll come back at the end to create our own *Family Definition* of Kindness.

Learn

Every family speaks love a little differently.

Dr. Gary Chapman teaches about *The Five Love Languages*—five simple ways people feel most loved.

They are:

- Words of Affirmation—Kind words and encouragement
- Quality Time—Being together without distractions
- Gifts—Thoughtful surprises or treats
- Acts of Service—Helping out and doing things for others
- Physical Touch—Hugs, high fives, sitting close

When we learn each other's love language, we can show kindness in a way that really matters.

Communicating with kindness is not just about what we say—it's how we show love every day.

Consider

Have you ever done something loving for someone, but it didn't seem to mean much to them?

Or has someone done something small for you that meant *everything*?

That's the power of love languages—we all feel loved in different ways.

Learning this helps families love each other *better*, not just *more*.

Let's Make It Real

As a family, take the free love languages quiz at:

www.5lovelanguages.com

After everyone finds their love language, share:

- What did you learn about yourself?
- What surprised you about someone else's love language?

Then answer together:

What could we do to show love in each other's love language this week?

Discuss

Go around the family and share your thoughts:

- Why is it helpful to know each other's love language?
- How can kindness look different for different people?
- What are some simple ways we can speak each other's love language every day?

Do

This week, practise speaking each other's love language:

- Look for ways to show love in the way that matters most to each person.
- Say thank you when someone does something kind—even if it's not *your* love language.
- Encourage each other to keep practising kindness in small ways.

End-of-Week Reflection

Gather as a family and talk about:

- What did we learn about our family's love languages this week?
- Did anyone feel extra loved because of something kind that happened?
- What will we keep doing to communicate kindness in ways that really count?

Family Definition

As a family, agree together:

What do we want the word 'Kindness' to mean in our home?

Write your family definition here:

_____

_____

_____

_____

WEEK 5:

SOLVING FAMILY PROBLEMS TOGETHER

"In this family, we solve problems together—because teamwork makes us stronger."

Key Word: Problem-Solving

Ask your family:

"What do you think the words 'Problem-Solving' mean?"

Talk about what makes a good problem-solver.

We'll come back at the end to create our own *Family Definition* of Problem-Solving.

Learn

Every family has problems—that's normal.

What makes families strong is learning to solve problems *together*—in a way that keeps everyone feeling heard, respected, and loved.

In this family, when we have a problem, we stop and GROW through it!

Our GROW Steps

G—Goal

What do we want to happen? What's the best outcome for everyone?

R—Roadblocks

What's getting in the way? What's tricky or causing the problem?

O—Options

What are all the ideas we can think of? Be creative—even silly ideas help us think outside the box.

W—Way Forward

What plan are we going to implement that's best for our family?

Consider

Have you ever been in a family argument where people just wanted to "win"?

Or have you been part of a family conversation where everyone worked together to find a solution?

Solving problems well makes our family feel safe, strong, and connected.

Let's Make It Real

Choose a small problem from your home life (bedtime routines, screen time, cleaning up toys, chores, getting ready in the morning).

As a family, talk it through using the *GROW* Steps.

Discuss

Pick one or two questions to start your conversation:

- Why is it important to solve problems kindly and together?
- What happens when families only focus on blaming or arguing?
- What could we do better when solving problems at home?
- When would using the GROW steps help us most?

Do

This week, practise using the GROW Problem-Solving Steps:

G—Goal: What do we want to happen?

R—Roadblocks: What's getting in the way?

O—Options: What are all the ideas we can think of? (even the crazy ones!)

W—Way Forward: What is the way forward from here?

End-of-Week Reflection

Gather as a family and talk about:

- Did we use the GROW method this week?
- How did it feel to work together as a family?
- What will we keep doing to become a family who solves problems in a loving way?

Family Definition

As a family, agree together:

What do we want the word 'Problem Solving' to mean in our home?

Write your family definition here:

_____

_____

_____

_____

WEEK 6:

RESPECTING EACH FAMILY MEMBER

"In this family, we show respect—because every person is valuable."

Key Word: Respect

Ask your family:

"What do you think the word 'Respect' means?"

Talk about what respect looks like at home and why it matters.

We'll come back at the end to create our own *Family Definition* of Respect.

Learn

Respect is how we show love in everyday moments.

In a family, respect sounds like:

- Using kind words
- Listening to each other
- Giving space when someone needs it
- Taking care of shared spaces
- Saying sorry when we need to

Respect doesn't mean we agree on everything—it means we care enough to treat each other well, even when we're different.

Consider

Every family has moments where respect can be hard—when we feel tired, annoyed, or frustrated.

But think about this:

Have you ever felt upset because someone didn't respect your space, feelings, or things?

Or have you felt really loved when someone treated you with extra care and kindness?

Respect is what makes home feel safe.

Let's Make It Real

Ask everyone to share a story or example:

Tell us about a time when you felt really respected at home. What happened?

Then share:

What's tricky about showing respect in our family every day?

Discuss

Take turns answering these:

- Why is respect important in a family?
- What does respect look like in our house?
- What happens when people feel disrespected at home?
- What could we practise this week to show more respect to each other?

Do

This week, notice how it feels when you:

- Use kind words, even when we feel upset
- Ask before using someone else's things
- Give space when someone needs quiet
- Say sorry when we forget to show respect

End-of-Week Reflection

Gather as a family and talk about:

- Did we notice respect growing in our family this week?
- What helped us show respect in tricky moments?
- What will we keep doing to stay a family who respects each other well?

Family Definition

As a family, agree together:

What do we want the word 'Respect' to mean in our home?

Write your family definition here:

_____

_____

_____

_____

WEEK 7:

BETTER TOGETHER AS A FAMILY

*"In this family, we're better together—we help,
we laugh, and we belong."*

Key Word: Teamwork

Ask your family:

"What do you think the word 'Teamwork' means?"

Share stories of when working together felt really good.

We'll come back at the end to create our own *Family Definition* of
Teamwork.

Learn

Every family is made up of different people—different personalities,
strengths, and ideas.

That's what makes a family special!

Strong families know they are *better together* because they:

- Share jobs and help each other
- Celebrate each person's strengths
- Support each other when life is hard
- Have more fun when they work as a team

Together is where family love grows.

Consider

Sometimes it feels easier to do things on our own or only care about what *we* need.

But think about this:

Have you ever been part of a team or family moment where working together made everything better?

Or have you seen what happens when everyone only thinks about themselves?

Family is strongest when we think *we,* not *me.*

Let's Make It Real

Go around the family and talk about:

Tell us about a time when we worked really well as a team at home. What happened?

Then share:

What's tricky about working together in our family? (e.g., sharing jobs, helping without being asked, staying kind when tired)

Discuss

Choose a few of these questions as a family:

- Why is family teamwork important?
- What does it feel like when everyone helps out and supports each other?
- What happens when we only think about ourselves?
- What could we practise this week to become a better team at home?

Do

Try this as a family together, this week:

- Look for a family job that needs everyone's help (e.g., cleaning up, cooking dinner, a family project).
- Share the load and cheer each other on.
- Celebrate how working together makes things easier and more fun.

End-of-Week Reflection

Gather as a family and talk about:

- Did we work together as a family team this week?
- What helped us be better together?

- What will we keep doing to stay a family that supports, helps, and enjoys being a team?

Family Definition

As a family, agree together:

What do we want the word 'Teamwork' to mean in our home?

Write your family definition here:

_____

_____

_____

_____

WEEK 8:

BUILDING TRUST AT HOME

"In this family, we build trust every day—by being honest, kind, and reliable."

Key Word: Trust

Ask your family:

"What do you think the word 'Trust' means?"

Talk about how trust is built or broken.

We'll come back at the end to create our own *Family Definition* of Trust.

Learn

Trust is like the glue that holds a family together.

Trust grows when we:

- Keep our promises
- Tell the truth
- Do what we say we'll do
- Show up for each other again and again

Trust doesn't happen all at once—it's built in little moments every day.

And once we have trust, we feel safe, close, and connected.

Consider

Have you ever trusted someone because they always showed up for you?

Or have you ever felt upset because trust was broken—maybe someone didn't do what they promised?

Trust is precious—it takes time to build but can break easily.

Strong families practise building and protecting trust every day.

Let's Make It Real

Encourage everyone to share their thoughts:

Tell us about a time when someone really earned your trust. What did they do?

Then share:

What do we find tricky about building or protecting trust in our family? (e.g., forgetting promises, not following through, not telling the truth)

Discuss

Let everyone have a turn sharing:

- Why is trust important in a family?
- What helps us build trust with each other?
- What can damage trust at home?
- What could we practise this week to build or protect trust as a family?

Do

This week, find ways to:

- Keep your promises—even the small ones.
- Be honest, even when it's hard.
- Say sorry if you break trust—and work to repair it.

Look for small ways to show you can be trusted.

End-of-Week Reflection

Gather as a family and talk about:

- Did we build trust with each other this week?
- What did we notice about how trust feels in our home?
- What will we keep doing to stay a family that protects trust?

Family Definition

As a family, agree together:

What do we want the word 'Trust' to mean in our home?

Write your family definition here:

_____

_____

_____

_____

WEEK 9:

BALANCING RESPONSIBILITY AND CONNECTION

"In this family, we work hard and love well—because both matter."

Key Word: Responsibility

Ask your family:

"What do you think the word 'Responsibility' means?"

Share ideas of what it looks like to be responsible.

We'll come back at the end to create our own *Family Definition* of Responsibility.

Learn

Every family needs both *responsibility* and *connection* to stay strong.

Responsibility is about:

- Doing your part
- Owning your actions
- Following through on what you said you'd do

Connection is about:

- Being kind
- Spending time together
- Showing love and care

If we only focus on responsibility, family life feels like a chore.

If we only focus on connection, things get messy and people feel frustrated.

A healthy family balances *both*.

Consider

Have you ever been in a family situation where people did their jobs, but no one felt close or connected?

Or have you been in a moment where you felt loved, but no one was doing what needed to be done?

The best families work together, show kindness, and take responsibility.

Let's Make It Real

Ask everyone to share a story or example:

Tell us about a time when our family felt really balanced––when everyone was doing their part *and* we felt connected.

Then share:

What's tricky about balancing responsibility and connection in our home? (e.g., feeling like one person is doing all the jobs, getting frustrated, forgetting to be kind when busy)

Discuss

Encourage everyone to share their ideas:

- Why do families need both responsibility and connection?
- What happens when we forget one of them?
- How can we help each other stay balanced?
- What could we practise this week to grow in both areas?

Do

This week, challenge yourself balancing responsibility and connection at home:

- When you do your jobs, do them with kindness and joy.
- When you spend time together, check if everyone's part is done first.
- Encourage each other with kind words when you notice someone being responsible.

End-of-Week Reflection

Gather as a family and talk about:

- Did we practise balancing responsibility and connection this week?

- What helped us do this well?
- What will we keep doing to stay a family who works hard *and* loves well?

Family Definition

As a family, agree together:

What do we want the word 'Responsibility' to mean in our home?

Write your family definition here:

_____

_____

_____

_____

WEEK 10:

EMPOWERING FAMILY MEMBERS WITH THE EMPOWERMENT MODEL

"In this family, we support each other to grow—not to rescue, but to empower."

Key Word: Empower

Ask your family:

"What do you think the word 'Empower' means?"

Talk about how we can help each other grow stronger.

We'll come back at the end to create our own *Family Definition* of Empower.

Learn

Empowering someone means helping them find their own answers-- not taking over or fixing things for them.

In our family, we want to support each other with love and respect, helping each person grow strong and confident.

We can do this by using the *Empowerment Model*—a 6-step way to help someone solve a problem without rescuing or controlling.

The Empowerment Model Steps

Empathy: Start by showing care--"Oh no! That sounds tricky."

Empower: Ask a powerful question--"What are you going to do about it?"

Explore: Get them thinking--"What have you already tried?"

Educate: Offer ideas if invited--"I have some ideas if you want to hear them."

Expect: Encourage ownership--"What's your plan from here?"

Encourage: Cheer them on--"Let me know how it goes. I believe in you!"

Consider

Have you ever had someone fix a problem *for* you—but it made you feel small or unimportant?

Or have you had someone walk beside you—asking good questions and letting you decide—and you felt proud and strong?

Empowering others helps them grow.

Let's Make It Real

Go around the family and answer:

Tell us about a time when someone supported you without taking over. How did that feel?

Then share:

What's tricky about not jumping in to rescue or control when someone has a problem?

Discuss

Ask these questions and listen well:

- Why is it important to empower each other in our family?
- What happens when we take over instead of support?
- How could using the Empowerment Model help us grow stronger together?

Do

This week, see what happens when you use the *Empowerment Model* when someone has a problem.

Empathy: Show care.

Empower: Ask "What are you going to do?"

Explore: Ask what they've already tried.

Educate: Offer ideas if asked.

Expect: Ask "What's your plan?"

Encourage: Cheer them on.

Notice how this helps people feel strong, not controlled.

End-of-Week Reflection

Gather as a family and talk about:

- Did we use the Empowerment Model with each other this week?
- How did it feel to be supported instead of rescued?
- What will we keep doing to stay a family who empowers each other?

Family Definition

As a family, agree together:

What do we want the word 'Empower' to mean in our home?

Write your family definition here:

_____

_____

_____

_____

PART TWO

EMPOWERING JOYFUL RESPONSIBILITY

In this section, your family will discover that taking responsibility for your actions doesn't need to feel like a burden—it can be empowering and joyful! Through relatable examples, practical activities, and thoughtful discussions, your family will explore responsibility as making mindful choices, understanding personal accountability, and recognizing how individual actions impact everyone around you.

Family members will learn to embrace responsibility with confidence, seeing it as an opportunity to contribute positively to family life and personal growth. By pursuing joyful responsibility, your family will build trust, strengthen connections, and nurture an environment where everyone feels valued and empowered.

WEEK 11:

OWNING YOUR CHOICES AT HOME

"In this family, we own our choices—and we learn from them."

Key Word: Choices

Ask your family:

"What do you think the word 'Choices' means?"

Talk about how our choices shape our day and our relationships.

We'll come back at the end to create our own *Family Definition* of Choices.

Learn

Every day we make choices—some big, some small.

In our family, we want to practise taking responsibility for our choices—not blaming others, making excuses, or pretending it's not our fault.

Owning your choices means:

- Admitting when you've made a mistake
- Saying sorry without blaming anyone else
- Choosing to fix what you can
- Learning and doing better next time

Powerful people take ownership of their actions—even when it's hard.

Consider

Have you ever felt tempted to blame someone else when things went wrong?

Or have you ever felt proud because you took responsibility and fixed something—even though it was tricky?

Families feel safe when everyone owns their part.

Let's Make It Real

Let everyone have a turn sharing:

Tell us about a time when you felt powerful because you took responsibility for your actions.

Then share:

What's tricky about owning your choices in our family?

(E.g., feeling embarrassed, not wanting to get in trouble, blaming others)

Discuss

Choose a few of these questions as a family:

- Why is it important to own our choices in a family?
- What happens when we blame others or avoid responsibility?
- What helps us practise being powerful people who own our actions?

Do

This week, see what happens when:

- You make a mistake, own it straight away.
- Say sorry without blaming anyone else.
- Ask, "What can I do to fix this?"
- Celebrate when someone takes ownership in a powerful way.

End-of-Week Reflection

Gather as a family and talk about:

- Did anyone practise owning their choices this week?
- How did it feel to take responsibility—even when it was hard?
- What will we keep doing to stay a family who owns our actions with courage?

Family Definition

As a family, agree together:

What do we want the word 'Choices' to mean in our home?

Write your family definition here:

_____

_____

_____

_____

WEEK 12:

POWERFUL FAMILIES CREATE POWERFUL CONNECTIONS

"In this family, we lead ourselves first—because powerful people choose love and respect."

Key Word: Powerful

Ask your family:

"What do you think the word 'Powerful' means?"

Talk about the difference between controlling others and controlling yourself.

We'll come back at the end to create our own *Family Definition* of Powerful.

Learn

In every relationship—including families—there are two ways people can act: *powerful* or *powerless*.

Powerful people:

- Take responsibility for themselves
- Manage their words, actions, and emotions
- Respect others without controlling them

Powerless people:

- Blame others for how they feel
- Try to control people or situations
- Avoid responsibility for their actions

In our family, we want to be powerful people—not because we control others—but because we control ourselves.

When everyone in a family acts powerfully, connection grows stronger and home feels safe.

Consider

Have you ever seen someone try to control others because they were feeling powerless?

Or have you seen someone stay calm, kind, and responsible even when things were hard?

Powerful people create peaceful homes.

Let's Make It Real

Invite each person to share:

Tell us about a time when you acted like a powerful person at home. What did you do?

Then share:

What's tricky about being powerful in our family—especially when we feel frustrated or upset?

Discuss

Explore these questions together as a family:

- What does it look like to be a powerful person at home?
- What happens when people act powerless in a family?
- How can we practise being powerful people this week—no matter what others are doing?

Do

This week, practise being a powerful person at home:

- Take responsibility for yourself—even when others don't.
- Speak kindly and calmly when you feel upset.
- Show respect to everyone—even in hard moments.
- Celebrate when family members act powerfully.

End-of-Week Reflection

Gather as a family and talk about:

- Did anyone act like a powerful person this week?
- How did it feel to control yourself instead of trying to control others?
- What will we keep doing to stay a family of powerful people who create connection?

Family Definition

As a family, agree together:

What do we want the word 'Powerful' to mean in our home?

Write your family definition here:

_____

_____

_____

_____

WEEK 13:

CHOOSING LOVE OVER FEAR

"In this family, we choose love—even when fear feels easier."

Key Word: Love

Ask your family:

"What do you think the word 'Love' means?"

Share ideas about what love looks like in action.

We'll come back at the end to create our own *Family Definition* of Love.

Learn

Every day in family life, we have a choice—to respond from *love* or to react from *fear*.

Fear makes us:

- Try to control others
- Avoid hard conversations
- Hide mistakes
- Distance ourselves from people

Love helps us:

- Build connection
- Tell the truth
- Be kind and brave
- Stay close—even in hard moments

Fear pushes people away.

Love brings people together.

Consider

Have you ever reacted out of fear—yelling, blaming, or shutting down—and it made things worse?

Or have you chosen love—staying calm, speaking kindly, being honest—and it made things better?

Choosing love is the most powerful thing we can do in our family.

Let's Make It Real

Ask everyone to share a story or example:

Tell us about a time when you reacted out of fear. What happened?

Then share:

Tell us about a time when you chose love. What was different?

Discuss

Talk about these questions together:

- What happens in a family when people react out of fear?
- What changes when we choose love instead?
- What could we practise this week to respond from love, even when fear tries to take over?

Do

Work together as a family this week to:

- Take a breath before reacting in tricky moments.
- Speak calmly instead of shouting or blaming.
- Be honest and kind—even when it feels hard.
- Celebrate every time someone chooses love.

Notice how choosing love makes home feel safer and closer.

End-of-Week Reflection

Gather as a family and talk about:

- Did we practise choosing love over fear this week?
- How did it feel to stay calm and connected in tricky moments?
- What will we keep doing to stay a family who chooses love first?

Family Definition

As a family, agree together:

What do we want the word 'Love' to mean in our home?

Write your family definition here:

_____

_____

_____

_____

WEEK 14:

SETTING HEALTHY FAMILY BOUNDARIES

"In this family, we set boundaries—because love
needs safety and respect."

Key Word: Boundaries

Ask your family:

"What do you think the word 'Boundaries' means?"

Talk about why boundaries help people feel safe and cared for.

We'll come back at the end to create our own *Family Definition* of
Boundaries.

Learn

Boundaries help keep our family safe, kind, and connected.

Healthy boundaries are like gentle fences—they show where my responsibility ends and yours begins.

Boundaries tell us:

- What is okay
- What is not okay
- How we will treat each other
- What I will do to take care of myself

Boundaries help us love well—without controlling or hurting each other.

Consider

Have you ever had a moment where someone crossed your boundary—maybe by yelling, grabbing, or not listening—and it didn't feel good?

Or have you set a boundary and felt safe and respected?

Boundaries protect relationships—they don't ruin them.

Let's Make It Real

Go around the family and talk about:

A time when a boundary helped you feel safe or loved.

Then share:

What do we find tricky about setting or respecting boundaries in our family?

(E.g., saying no kindly, not pushing someone when they need space)

Discuss

Use these questions to guide your family conversation:

- Why do healthy boundaries matter in a family?
- What happens when boundaries aren't clear or respected?
- What boundaries would help our family stay kind, respectful, and connected?

Do

This week, practise setting and respecting healthy boundaries at home:

- Be clear and kind when setting a boundary: "I'm not okay with being spoken to like that."
- Respect other people's boundaries—even if they're different to yours.
- Notice when boundaries help solve problems kindly.

You might even create a simple *Family Boundary List* together like:

- We speak kindly—no shouting or name-calling.
- We knock before entering bedrooms.
- We take a break when we feel upset.

End-of-Week Reflection

Gather as a family and talk about:

- Did we practise setting or respecting boundaries this week?
- How did boundaries help us feel safer or more connected?

- What will we keep doing to stay a family who uses healthy boundaries with love?

Family Definition

As a family, agree together:

What do we want the word 'Boundaries' to mean in our home?

Write your family definition here:

_____

_____

_____

_____

WEEK 15:

PROTECTING AND STRENGTHENING FAMILY CONNECTION

"In this family, we protect connection—because people matter more than problems."

Key Word: Connection

Ask your family:

"What do you think the word 'Connection' means?"

Talk about what helps you feel close to people at home.

We'll come back at the end to create our own *Family Definition* of Connection.

Learn

Every family needs connection—it's the invisible string that ties us together.

Connection makes home feel safe, warm, and welcoming.

Disconnection makes home feel tense, lonely, or frustrating.

Every day, our words and actions either *strengthen* connection or *weaken* it.

Things that *strengthen* connection:

- Listening properly (without interrupting or looking at devices)
- Speaking kindly and calmly
- Saying thank you and noticing each other's effort
- Spending time together without distractions
- Saying sorry when we've messed up
- Respecting space and boundaries
- Helping out without being asked

Things that *weaken* connection:

- Yelling or using harsh words
- Ignoring people or giving silent treatment
- Walking away mid-conversation
- Rolling eyes, huffing, or using rude body language
- Not owning mistakes
- Blaming or shaming each other

Connection is like a rope—the more we take care of it, the stronger it gets.

But if we ignore it, pull it too hard, or neglect it, it can feel fragile and frayed.

In our family, we want to practise *protecting connection*—especially in hard moments.

Consider

Encourage everyone to share their thoughts:

Tell us about a time when you felt really connected to someone at home. What happened?

Then share:

What do we find tricky about protecting connection in our family every day?

(E.g., being busy, getting frustrated, forgetting to listen)

Discuss

Go around the family and share your thoughts:

- Why is connection so important in a family?
- What helps you feel most connected at home?
- What do we do (even without realising) that weakens connection?
- What could we practise this week to build connection together?

Do

Find ways this week to:

- Listen properly to each other.

- Look for small ways to connect—a game, a story, a walk, sitting together.
- Speak kindly—even when you feel tired or frustrated.
- Say sorry quickly if you've hurt connection.

Notice how connection grows stronger with small daily actions.

End-of-Week Reflection

Gather as a family and talk about:

- What moments helped us feel connected this week?
- What did we do that helped protect connection?
- What will we keep doing to stay a family who builds and protects connection every day?

Family Definition

As a family, agree together:

What do we want the word 'Connection' to mean in our home?

Write your family definition here:

_____

_____

_____

_____

WEEK 16:

GROWING RESPONSIBILITY TOGETHER

"In this family, we all do our part—because responsibility
helps us care for what matters most."

Key Word: Ownership

Start by asking everyone in the family:

"What do you think the word 'Ownership' means?"

Talk about how ownership is more than doing jobs—it's about taking care of what belongs to you: your words, your actions, your choices, your space, and your part in family life.

Ask:

- What does it look like when someone takes ownership?
- What happens when people avoid ownership?

Listen to each other's ideas—we'll come back at the end to create our own *Family Definition* of Ownership.

Learn

Responsibility is not just about doing jobs or chores—it's about growing into someone who can be trusted to care for themselves, their words, their actions, and the people around them.

In healthy families, responsibility is *shared*.

We all have a part to play in making home a peaceful, safe, and happy place.

Responsibility shows up in small everyday choices like:

- Remembering what's yours to do
- Owning your actions (without blaming anyone else)
- Helping out without waiting to be asked
- Looking after your own belongings
- Being honest and following through on your word
- Admitting mistakes and making it right

Responsibility isn't about being perfect—it's about growing.

The more responsibility we carry well, the more trust we build.

Consider

Have you ever felt proud because you were trusted with something important?

Or have you seen what happens when someone avoids responsibility—and others have to pick up their part?

Families who share responsibility build trust, teamwork, and connection.

Let's Make It Real

Take turns answering these questions:

Tell us about a time when you were trusted with something important—how did it feel?

Then share:

What is tricky about taking responsibility in our family?

(E.g., remembering things, getting distracted, wanting to avoid jobs)

Discuss

Pick one or two questions to start your conversation:

- Why is responsibility important in a family?
- What happens when someone avoids responsibility?
- How does taking responsibility help us trust and rely on each other more?
- What could we practise this week to grow responsibility together?

Do

Throughout the week, look for ways to:

- Choose one area where you want to take more ownership (a job, a habit, a space).
- Help out without being reminded.
- Be honest and own your actions straight away.
- Celebrate when family members take responsibility in a powerful way.

End-of-Week Reflection

Gather as a family and talk about:

- Did we practise growing responsibility together this week?
- What helped us take ownership well?
- What will we keep doing to stay a family who grows responsibility with trust and care?

Family Definition

As a family, agree together:

What do we want the word 'Ownership' to mean in our home?

Write your family definition here:

_____

_____

_____

_____

WEEK 17:

LEARNING FROM MISTAKES AS A FAMILY

"In this family, mistakes are for learning—not for hiding."

Key Word: Mistakes

Start by asking everyone in the family:

"What do you think the word 'Mistakes' means?"

Take turns sharing your thoughts—there's no right or wrong answer.

Listen to each other and notice how different people think about this word.

We'll come back to this at the end to create our own *Family Definition* of Mistakes.

Learn

Every family makes mistakes—that's normal and part of growing.

What matters most is what happens *after* a mistake. Do we hide it? Blame someone else? Or do we own it and learn from it?

Mistakes are actually an important part of learning. They help us:

- Grow stronger
- Get better at new things
- Take responsibility for our actions
- Restore connection with each other

In this family, we want to say:

"It's okay to make mistakes—but let's learn from them."

Love gives us freedom. Freedom gives us choices. And one of those choices is learning from what didn't go well.

Consider

Go around the family and answer:

Tell us about a time when you made a mistake—and you learned something really valuable from it.

Then share:

What is tricky about admitting mistakes in our family?

(E.g., feeling embarrassed, fear of getting in trouble, wanting to hide it)

Discuss

Take turns answering these:

- Why is it important to create a family where mistakes lead to learning?
- What happens when mistakes are met with fear or punishment?
- What could we practise this week to handle mistakes better at home?

Do

This week, practise being a family who learns from mistakes:

- When you make a mistake, own it quickly.
- Ask, "What can I learn from this?"
- Be kind and gentle when someone else makes a mistake.
- Celebrate when mistakes turn into learning moments.

End-of-Week Reflection

Gather as a family and talk about:

- Did we practise learning from mistakes this week?
- What helped us handle mistakes well?
- What will we keep doing to stay a family who sees mistakes as part of learning and growing?

Family Definition

As a family, agree together:

What do we want the word 'Mistakes' to mean in our home?

Write your family definition here:

_____

_____

_____

_____

WEEK 18:

HELPING EACH OTHER GROW AT HOME

"In this family, we help each other grow—because we're better when we grow together."

Key Word: Growth

Start by asking everyone in the family:

"What do you think the word 'Growth' means?"

Talk about how growth isn't just about getting taller or older—it's about learning, improving, and becoming a better version of ourselves.

Ask:

- What helps people grow?
- What stops people from growing?

Listen to each other's ideas—we'll come back at the end to create our own *Family Definition* of Growth.

Learn

In a healthy family, everyone is growing.

Sometimes growth looks big—like learning a new skill or reaching a goal.

But often, growth looks small—like trying again, being kinder, or learning from mistakes.

As a family, we can help each other grow by:

- Encouraging effort, not just results
- Cheering each other on
- Giving helpful feedback
- Being patient when someone is learning
- Noticing the little wins
- Celebrating progress, not just perfection

Growth happens best when home is a safe place to try, fail, learn, and try again.

Consider

Go around the family and answer:

Tell us about a time when you grew in something—even if it was hard or slow.

Then share:

What helps us grow well in our family? What makes it hard to grow sometimes?

Discuss

Let everyone have a turn sharing:

- Why is growth important in a family?
- How do we show support when someone is learning or trying something new?
- What could we practise this week to create a home where growth happens often?

Do

This week, see what happens when you:

- Notice when someone tries hard—and encourage them.
- Celebrate progress—even if it's small.
- Be patient with yourself and others.
- Share one thing you're working on growing in right now.

You might even create a *Family Growth Wall* where you write or draw things you see each other growing in.

End-of-Week Reflection

Gather as a family and talk about:

- How did we help each other grow this week?
- What made it easier to keep learning and trying?
- What will we keep doing to stay a family who encourages growth?

Family Definition

As a family, agree together:

What do we want the word 'Growth' to mean in our home?

Write your family definition here:

_____

_____

_____

_____

WEEK 19:

RESILIENCE: STICKING WITH IT AS A FAMILY

"In this family, we don't give up—we grow stronger."

Key Word: Resilience

Start by asking everyone in the family:

"What do you think the word 'Resilience' means?"

Talk about how resilience is what helps us bounce back, keep going, and stay strong when things get hard.

Ask:

- What does resilience look like in everyday life?
- When do people need resilience the most?

Listen to each other's ideas—we'll come back at the end to create our own *Family Definition* of Resilience.

Learn

Every family faces challenges—hard days, disappointments, mistakes, and moments where we feel like giving up.

Resilience is what helps us:

- Keep trying
- Stay calm under pressure
- Be flexible when things don't go to plan
- Learn from failure
- Stick together as a family even when life feels hard

Resilience doesn't mean things are always easy—it means we don't quit when things are hard.

Resilient families know that the tough times won't last—but strong relationships will.

Consider

Ask everyone to share a story or exampler:

Tell us about a time when you had to be resilient—when something was really hard but you didn't give up.

Then share:

What helps us build resilience in our family? What makes it tricky?

Discuss

Encourage everyone to share their ideas:

- Why is resilience important in a family?
- How do we help each other stay strong when things feel hard?
- What could we practise this week to grow resilience together?

Do

Do this together as a family:

- Notice when someone is trying really hard—and encourage them.
- Remind each other that hard things don't last forever.
- Talk about past family challenges you've overcome together.
- Celebrate effort and courage—not just success.

End-of-Week Reflection

Gather as a family and talk about:

- Did we practise resilience this week?
- What helped us stick with things when it felt hard?
- What will we keep doing to stay a family who is strong, flexible, and resilient?

Family Definition

As a family, agree together:

What do we want the word 'Resilience' to mean in our home?

Write your family definition here:

_____

_____

_____

_____

WEEK 20:

JOYFUL RESPONSIBILITY AT HOME

"In this family, we take responsibility with a joyful heart—because helping each other makes us strong."

Key Word: Joyful

Start by asking everyone in the family:

"What do you think the word 'Joyful' means?"

Talk about how joy is more than just feeling happy—it's choosing to have a good attitude, even when things aren't perfect.

Ask:

- What does being joyful look like at home?
- How is joy different from just feeling happy?

Listen to each other's ideas—we'll come back at the end to create our own *Family Definition* of Joyful.

Learn

Joyful responsibility is about doing what needs to be done—with a good attitude.

In every family, there are things we *have* to do—like chores, helping out, and getting ready on time.

But the attitude we choose while we do those things makes a big difference.

Being joyful looks like:

- Smiling while helping out
- Speaking kindly while doing your job
- Having fun while working together
- Encouraging others
- Choosing a good attitude—even when you don't feel like it

Joy in a family makes home feel lighter, warmer, and more fun.

Consider

Go around the family and talk about:

Tell us about a time when you chose to do something with joy—and it made the moment better for everyone.

Then share:

What is tricky about being joyful when we're doing something we don't feel like doing?

Discuss

Ask these questions and listen well:

- Why is joy important in family life?
- What happens when everyone works with a grumpy attitude?
- What could we practise this week to bring more joy into our responsibilities at home?

Do

Challenge yourself this week to:

- Smile while doing jobs.
- Speak kindly to each other during routines and chores.
- Put on music while cleaning up.
- Encourage each other to choose joy.

You might even create a *Family Joy Jar*—where you write down fun or silly ideas to make jobs more joyful together.

End-of-Week Reflection

Gather as a family and talk about:

- Did we practise joyful responsibility this week?
- What helped us choose a good attitude?
- What will we keep doing to stay a family who brings joy into everyday life?

Family Definition

As a family, agree together:

What do we want the word 'Joyful' to mean in our home?

Write your family definition here:

_____

_____

_____

_____

PART THREE

PURSUING GENUINE RESTORATION

In this section, your family will focus on understanding the value of restoration when conflicts or misunderstandings arise. You'll explore the importance of sincere apologies, forgiveness, and proactive efforts to rebuild trust and heal relationships.

Through meaningful conversations, reflective activities, and practical strategies, family members will learn to approach restoration with honesty, humility, and care. Embracing genuine restoration practices ensures your family relationships remain resilient, supportive, and loving, even through difficult moments.

WEEK 21:

THE ART OF APOLOGY AT HOME

"In this family, we say sorry well—and we work to make things right."

Key Word: Restoration

Start by asking everyone in the family:

"What do you think the word 'Restoration' means?"

Talk about how restoration is about fixing what's been broken—not just saying sorry, but making things right again.

Ask:

- What does restoration look like in a family?
- Why is it important to restore connection after a mistake or hurt?

Listen to each other's ideas—we'll come back at the end to create our own *Family Definition* of Restoration.

Learn

Everyone makes mistakes—but in strong families, we learn the art of apology and restoration.

A real apology is not just words—it's about fixing what's broken.

Restoration means:

- Owning what you did wrong
- Saying sorry with a genuine heart
- Asking, "What can I do to make it right?"
- Changing your actions going forward
- Restoring connection, not just fixing the problem

When we practise restoration at home, we protect trust, respect, and connection.

Consider

Encourage everyone to share their thoughts:

Tell us about a time when someone gave you a real apology, and it made things feel better.

Then share:

What is tricky about saying sorry properly in our family?

(E.g., feeling embarrassed, wanting to avoid it, blaming others)

Discuss

Choose a few of these questions as a family:

- Why is restoration important in family life?
- What happens when people say sorry but don't change their actions?
- What could we practise this week to become a family who restores connection well?

Do

During your week together, focus on:

- If you hurt someone, own it quickly.
- Say a real apology: "I'm sorry for…"
- Ask, "What can I do to make it right?"
- Show with your actions that you care about restoring trust and connection.

You might even create a *Family Restoration Plan*—what steps do we follow when someone says sorry?

End-of-Week Reflection

Gather as a family and talk about:

- Did we practise restoration well this week?
- What helped us fix things properly after mistakes?
- What will we keep doing to stay a family who values restoration?

Family Definition

As a family, agree together:

What do we want the word 'Restoration' to mean in our home?

Write your family definition here:

_____

_____

_____

_____

WEEK 22:

FORGIVENESS AND MOVING FORWARD AS A FAMILY

"In this family, we forgive—because holding
onto hurt hurts us too."

Key Word: Forgiveness

Start by asking everyone in the family:

"What do you think the word 'Forgiveness' means?"

Talk about how forgiveness is letting go of hurt or anger—not pretending it didn't happen, but choosing to move forward without holding onto it.

Ask:

- What does forgiveness look like in everyday family life?
- Why is forgiveness sometimes hard?

Listen to each other's ideas—we'll come back at the end to create our own *Family Definition* of Forgiveness.

Learn

Forgiveness is a gift we give to ourselves and to others.

It doesn't mean saying what happened was okay—it means choosing to let go of anger, blame, or punishment so that we can move forward.

Forgiveness helps us:

- Let go of heavy feelings
- Restore connection
- Free ourselves from bitterness
- Create peace in our hearts and home

Without forgiveness, families can stay stuck in hurt. With forgiveness, families move forward together.

Consider

Take turns answering these questions:

Tell us about a time when someone forgave you—or you forgave someone—and it helped restore peace.

Then share:

What is tricky about forgiveness in our family?

(E.g., holding onto hurt, wanting to stay angry, waiting for someone else to apologise first)

Discuss

Explore these questions together as a family:

- Why is forgiveness important in family life?
- What happens when people stay stuck in hurt or blame?
- What could we practise this week to forgive quickly and move forward well?

Do

This week, practise forgiveness at home:

- If you feel upset, talk about it kindly.
- Choose to forgive, even if someone hasn't said sorry yet.
- Let go of punishment or blame once an apology is made.
- Encourage each other when forgiveness feels hard.

End-of-Week Reflection

Gather as a family and talk about:

- Did we practise forgiveness well this week?
- What helped us move forward after hurt or mistakes?
- What will we keep doing to stay a family who forgives quickly and loves deeply?

Family Definition

As a family, agree together:

What do we want the word 'Forgiveness' to mean in our home?

Write your family definition here:

_____

_____

_____

_____

WEEK 23:

RESTORING FAMILY TRUST

"In this family, we build trust with honesty, kindness, and keeping our word."

Key Word: Trustworthiness

Start by asking everyone in the family:

"What do you think the word 'Trustworthiness' means?"

Talk about how trustworthiness is not just about being trusted once—it's about being reliable, honest, and consistent over time.

Ask:

- What does it look like when someone is trustworthy?
- Why does trust grow slowly but break quickly?

Listen to each other's ideas—we'll come back at the end to create our own *Family Definition* of Trustworthiness.

Learn

Trust is built in small, everyday moments.

Being trustworthy means people know they can count on you—that your words and actions line up.

In family life, we build trust by:

- Keeping our promises
- Telling the truth
- Owning mistakes
- Following through on what we said we'd do
- Showing kindness and respect even when no one is watching

Broken trust can always be restored—but it takes time, consistency, and patience.

Consider

Let everyone have a turn sharing:

Tell us about a time when you trusted someone—or someone trusted you—and it felt really good.

Then share:

What is tricky about rebuilding trust when it's been broken?

(E.g., waiting for someone to change, proving yourself again, being patient)

Discuss

Talk about these questions together:

- Why is trustworthiness important in family life?
- What helps trust grow strong at home?
- What could we practise this week to be trustworthy and to restore trust when needed?

Do

See what happens when you:

- Follow through on promises—even small ones.
- Be honest—even when it's hard.
- Apologise and take action when trust is broken.
- Encourage each other when trust is being rebuilt.

You might even create a *Family Trust List*—things we all agree help trust grow strong in our home.

End-of-Week Reflection

Gather as a family and talk about:

- Did we practise trustworthiness this week?
- What helped us restore or build trust?
- What will we keep doing to stay a family who values trust and works to restore it well?

Family Definition

As a family, agree together:

What do we want the word 'Trustworthiness' to mean in our home?

Write your family definition here:

_____

_____

_____

_____

WEEK 24:

GIVING SECOND CHANCES

"In this family, we give grace—because we all need it."

Key Word: Grace

Start by asking everyone in the family:

"What do you think the word 'Grace' means?"

Talk about how grace is when we choose to treat someone with kindness, patience, and forgiveness—even when they don't deserve it.

Ask:

- What does grace look like in everyday family life?
- How does grace make home feel safe and loving?

Listen to each other's ideas—we'll come back at the end to create our own *Family Definition* of Grace.

Learn

Grace is a powerful choice we make in family life.

It means offering people a second chance—not because they earned it, but because we love them and want connection more than punishment.

Grace is not ignoring mistakes—it's choosing kindness *while* we help people grow and learn.

Grace in families looks like:

- Being patient when someone is still learning
- Offering a second chance after a mistake
- Speaking kindly even when we feel frustrated
- Helping someone start again without shame
- Remembering we all need grace sometimes

Consider

Go around the family and answer:

Tell us about a time when someone gave you grace—and it helped you feel safe or loved.

Then share:

What is tricky about showing grace in our family?

(E.g., feeling hurt, wanting to stay mad, finding it hard to let go)

Discuss

Use these questions to guide your family conversation:

- Why is grace important in family life?
- What happens when people don't offer second chances?
- What could we practise this week to be a family who shows grace well?

Do

This week, find ways to:

- Be patient with people who are still learning or growing.
- Offer a second chance after a mistake.
- Speak with kindness and encouragement when someone is trying again.
- Celebrate moments where grace made a big difference.

End-of-Week Reflection

Gather as a family and talk about:

- Did we practise grace well this week?
- What helped us offer second chances with kindness?
- What will we keep doing to stay a family who gives grace generously?

Family Definition

As a family, agree together:

What do we want the word 'Grace' to mean in our home?

Write your family definition here:

_____

_____

_____

_____

WEEK 25:

TAKING RESPONSIBILITY IN FAMILY RELATIONSHIPS

"In this family, we own our actions and help each other grow."

Key Word: Accountability

Start by asking everyone in the family:

"What do you think the word 'Accountability' means?"

Talk about how accountability is when we take ownership of our choices and allow others to support us in staying true to who we want to be.

Ask:

- What does accountability look like in our family?
- Why does accountability help relationships stay strong?

Listen to each other's ideas—we'll come back at the end to create our own *Family Definition* of Accountability.

Learn

Healthy families practise accountability.

That means taking responsibility for:

- Our words
- Our actions
- Our attitudes
- Our mistakes

Accountability also means being willing to:

- Admit when we are wrong
- Let others remind us of what's right
- Make things right when needed
- Ask for help when we need support

Accountability keeps relationships clear, honest, and connected.

Without accountability, people avoid ownership or blame others.

With accountability, people grow in trust and respect.

Consider

Ask everyone to share a story or example:

Tell us about a time when being accountable helped a situation go better—even if it was hard.

Then share:

What is tricky about accountability in our family?

(E.g., being honest, feeling embarrassed, wanting to hide mistakes)

Discuss

Go around the family and share your thoughts:

- Why is accountability important in family life?
- What happens when we avoid taking responsibility?
- What could we practise this week to grow accountability together?

Do

As a family, this week agree to:

- Own your words and actions straight away.
- Be honest about mistakes or struggles.
- Accept reminders or help from family members kindly.
- Celebrate when someone takes responsibility in a powerful way.

End-of-Week Reflection

Gather as a family and talk about:

- Did we practise accountability well this week?
- What helped us take responsibility in our relationships?
- What will we keep doing to stay a family who values accountability?

Family Definition

As a family, agree together:

What do we want the word 'Accountability' to mean in our home?

Write your family definition here:

_____

_____

_____

_____

WEEK 26:

BUILDING POWERFUL FAMILY BONDS

"In this family, you belong--just as you are."

Key Word: Belonging

Start by asking everyone in the family:

"What do you think the word 'Belonging' means?"

Talk about how belonging is feeling safe, loved, and accepted for who you are—knowing that you have a special place in your family.

Ask:

- What helps you feel like you belong in our family?
- What can make people feel left out or disconnected?

Listen to each other's ideas—we'll come back at the end to create our own *Family Definition* of Belonging.

Learn

Every person needs to feel like they belong.

Belonging is not about being perfect—it's about being known, accepted, and loved exactly as you are.

In our family, we build belonging by:

- Welcoming each other just as we are
- Listening and showing interest
- Including everyone
- Valuing our differences
- Making home a safe and loving place to be

When people feel they belong, they are more likely to:

- Be honest
- Take responsibility
- Stay connected
- Feel confident to grow

Consider

Encourage everyone to share their thoughts:

Tell us about a time when you really felt like you belonged somewhere—what made it special?

Then share:

What helps people feel like they belong in our family? What makes it harder?

Discuss

Pick one or two questions to start your conversation:

- Why is belonging important in family life?
- What happens when someone feels left out or disconnected?
- What could we practise this week to build belonging together?

Do

Notice how it feels when you:

- Look for ways to include everyone.
- Celebrate what makes each family member unique.
- Speak words that remind each other: "You belong here."
- Create a fun family tradition or routine that helps everyone feel connected.

End-of-Week Reflection

Gather as a family and talk about:

- Did we practise building belonging this week?
- What helped us feel more connected and safe?
- What will we keep doing to stay a family where everyone belongs?

Family Definition

As a family, agree together:

What do we want the word 'Belonging' to mean in our home?

Write your family definition here:

_____

_____

_____

_____

WEEK 27:

BECOMING A POWERFUL
FAMILY MEMBER

"In this family, we lead ourselves first—because powerful people create connection."

Key Word: Powerful Person

Start by asking everyone in the family:

"What do you think it means to be a 'Powerful Person'?"

Talk about how being powerful doesn't mean being bossy, controlling, or the loudest person in the room—it means being responsible for yourself and making choices that build connection.

Ask:

- What does a powerful person look like in our family?
- How do powerful people act differently to powerless people?

Listen to each other's ideas—we'll come back at the end to create our own *Family Definition* of Powerful Person.

Learn

Powerful people don't control others—they control themselves.

In our family, we want to grow as powerful people because powerful people:

1. Take responsibility for themselves
2. Manage their words, actions, and emotions
3. Show love and respect—even when life feels tricky

Powerless people blame, control, avoid, or wait for others to change.

Powerful people lead themselves first—and that makes home feel safer and stronger.

Being a powerful person looks like:

- Speaking kindly when upset
- Owning mistakes without excuses
- Making choices that protect connection
- Being responsible for your actions—even if others aren't

Consider

Take turns answering these questions:

Tell us about a time when you acted like a powerful person—what did you do that showed self-control or kindness?

Then share:

What is tricky about being a powerful person in our family?

(E.g., wanting to control others, blaming, feeling frustrated)

Discuss

Choose a few of these questions as a family:

- Why is being a powerful person important in family life?
- What happens when people act powerless or controlling?
- What could we practise this week to grow as powerful people together?

Do

Throughout the week, look for ways to:

- Take responsibility for your words and actions.
- Speak with kindness—even in hard moments.
- Manage your emotions—take a break if needed.
- Encourage others when you see them acting like a powerful person.

End-of-Week Reflection

Gather as a family and talk about:

- Did we practise being powerful people this week?
- What helped us lead ourselves well?
- What will we keep doing to stay a family of powerful people?

Family Definition

As a family, agree together:

What do we want the words 'Powerful Person' to mean in our home?

Write your family definition here:

_____

_____

_____

_____

WEEK 28:

RESTORING SELF-RESPECT

*"In this family, we respect ourselves because
we know we are valuable."*

Key Word: Self-Respect

Start by asking everyone in the family:

"What do you think the word 'Self-Respect' means?"

Talk about how self-respect is about knowing you are valuable, treating yourself kindly, and making choices that show you care about who you are becoming.

Ask:

- What does self-respect look like in everyday family life?
- What happens when someone forgets to respect him or herself?

Listen to each other's ideas—we'll come back at the end to create our own *Family Definition* of Self-Respect.

Learn

Self-respect is the way we show love and care to ourselves.

In a family, we want every person to feel valuable—not because of what they do—but because of who they are.

Practising self-respect looks like:

- Speaking kindly to yourself
- Taking care of your body and emotions
- Owning mistakes without shame
- Choosing friends and habits that are good for you
- Making choices that line up with your values

When we respect ourselves, we treat others with respect too.

Families who practise self-respect are stronger, healthier, and kinder—because they know their worth.

Consider

Let everyone have a turn sharing:

Tell us about a time when you showed self-respect. What did you do that was kind or caring toward yourself?

Then share:

What is tricky about showing self-respect at home?

(E.g., negative self-talk, copying others' bad habits, feeling not good enough)

Discuss

Take turns answering these:

- Why is self-respect important in family life?
- What happens when people forget their worth or value?
- What could we practise this week to grow in self-respect?

Do

Choose one moment each day to:

- Speak kindly about yourself.
- Take care of your space, your body, and your emotions.
- Make choices that are healthy and helpful for you.
- Encourage others when you see them showing self-respect.

End-of-Week Reflection

Gather as a family and talk about:

- Did we practise self-respect well this week?
- What helped us treat ourselves with kindness and care?
- What will we keep doing to stay a family who values self-respect?

Family Definition

As a family, agree together:

What do we want the words 'Self-Respect' to mean in our home?

Write your family definition here:

_____

_____

_____

_____

WEEK 29:

TAKING INITIATIVE USING THE EMPOWERMENT MODEL

"In this family, we don't wait for others—we lead ourselves first."

Key Word: Initiative

Start by asking everyone in the family:

"What do you think the word 'Initiative' means?"

Talk about how initiative means noticing what needs to be done, and doing it without being asked.

Ask:

- Why does taking initiative help a family?
- What happens when no one takes initiative?

Listen to each other's ideas—we'll come back at the end to create our own *Family Definition* of Initiative.

Learn

Initiative is when we take action—not because we are told, but because we care.

Sometimes in a family, we wait for someone else to fix a problem or help out. But powerful people practise initiative.

One way we can take initiative when solving problems is by using the *Empowerment Model*:

Empathy: Start by showing care--"Oh no! That sounds tricky."

Empower: Ask a powerful question--"What are you going to do about it?"

Explore: Get them thinking--"What have you already tried?"

Educate: Offer ideas if invited--"I have some ideas if you want to hear them."

Expect: Encourage ownership--"What's your plan from here?"

Encourage: Cheer them on--"Let me know how it goes. I believe in you!"

This model helps us support others to solve problems and take initiative—without controlling or rescuing them.

Consider

Invite each person to share:

Tell us about a time when you took initiative at home. How did it feel to act without being asked?

Then share:

What is tricky about taking initiative in our family?

(E.g., waiting for someone else, feeling nervous, not noticing)

Discuss

Let everyone have a turn sharing:

- Why is taking initiative important in family life?
- How does the Empowerment Model help us take action without controlling others?
- What could we practise this week to take initiative more often?

Do

This week, practise using the Empowerment Model at home:

- Look for small problems or needs, and take action.
- Use the steps of Empathy, Empower, Explore, Educate, Expect, Encourage.
- Be quick to help or lead yourself when you see something that needs to be done.

End-of-Week Reflection

Gather as a family and talk about:

- Did we practise taking initiative well this week?
- What helped us act without waiting to be asked?
- What will we keep doing to stay a family who takes initiative with love and responsibility?

Family Definition

As a family, agree together:

What do we want the word 'Initiative' to mean in our home?

Write your family definition here:

_____

_____

_____

_____

WEEK 30:

BEING A FAMILY ROLE MODEL

*"In this family, we influence others by how we live
—not just what we say."*

Key Word: Influence

Start by asking everyone in the family:

"What do you think the word 'Influence' means?"

Talk about how influence is the way we affect or inspire others—not just with our words, but with how we live every day.

Ask:

- Who has been a good influence in your life? Why?
- What kind of influence do we want to have in our family?

Listen to each other's ideas—we'll come back at the end to create our own *Family Definition* of Influence.

Learn

Everyone has influence, whether we realise it or not.

In our family, we influence each other through:

- Our attitudes
- Our actions
- Our words
- Our choices
- The example we set—even when no one is watching

Being a role model doesn't mean being perfect—it means being intentional about who we are becoming and how we treat others.

Good influence happens when we:

- Stay kind even in hard moments
- Practise responsibility
- Encourage others
- Make healthy choices
- Live in a way that others would want to follow

Consider

Ask everyone to share a story or example:

Tell us about a time when someone's good influence helped you grow or make a wise choice.

Then share:

What is tricky about being a good influence at home?

(E.g., getting frustrated, copying bad habits, forgetting people are watching)

Discuss

Encourage everyone to share their ideas:

- Why is influence important in family life?
- What happens when we forget we are influencing others?
- What could we practise this week to be a positive influence at home?

Do

Spend time this week practising:

- Choose your words carefully.
- Kindness and respect even in small moments.
- Notice and celebrate good influence when you see it.
- Ask yourself: "Would I want others to copy this choice?"

End-of-Week Reflection

Gather as a family and talk about:

- Did we practise positive influence well this week?
- What helped us be good role models at home?
- What will we keep doing to stay a family who uses influence for good?

Family Definition

As a family, agree together:

What do we want the word 'Influence' to mean in our home?

Write your family definition here:

_____

_____

_____

_____

PART FOUR

A CULTURE OF LOVE

In the final section, your family will deepen your understanding of what it means to build and sustain a culture of love. You'll engage in activities and reflections that emphasize empathy, compassion, kindness, and genuine appreciation for one another.

This section guides your family in creating a lasting environment where every member feels cherished, respected, and connected. By nurturing a culture of love, your family will develop strong emotional bonds and a positive, enduring legacy.

WEEK 31:

SERVICE AND CONTRIBUTION AT HOME

"In this family, we look for ways to help—because everyone has something valuable to give."

Key Word: Contribution

Start by asking everyone in the family:

"What do you think the word 'Contribution' means?"

Talk about how contribution means adding something good—your time, effort, or kindness—to help others.

Ask:

- What does contribution look like in our family?
- How does contribution make home or the world a better place?

Listen to each other's ideas—we'll come back at the end to create our own *Family Definition* of Contribution.

Learn

Every family has the chance to contribute—both inside the home and out in the community.

Contribution isn't about being perfect—it's about being willing to add value wherever you are.

In our family, contribution looks like:

- Helping each other without being asked
- Sharing our time, energy, or talents
- Thinking about others' needs—not just our own
- Serving our wider community in simple, practical ways

When we all contribute, family life feels lighter, more joyful, and more connected.

Consider

Go around the family and answer:

Tell us about a time when someone's contribution (big or small) made a difference to you.

Then share:

What is tricky about contributing well—either at home or in the community?

(E.g., feeling tired, not noticing needs, waiting for someone else to act)

Discuss

Choose a few of these questions as a family:

- Why is contribution important in family life?
- How do we feel when everyone shares the load and helps?
- What could we practise this week to become a family who contributes well?

Do

This week, practise contribution in two ways:

1. At home—look for ways to help each other without being asked.
2. In the community—agree on one simple act of service you could do together.

Ideas could include:

- Baking for a neighbour
- Donating items to a local charity
- Writing thank you cards for people in your school or community
- Helping clean up a park or street
- Offering to help someone in need

Choose something that fits your family and commit to doing it together this week.

End-of-Week Reflection

Gather as a family and talk about:

- Did we practise contribution well this week?

- What helped us focus on serving others?

- What will we keep doing to stay a family who contributes at home and in our community?

Family Definition

As a family, agree together:

What do we want the word 'Contribution' to mean in our home?

Write your family definition here:

_____

_____

_____

_____

WEEK 32:

MENTORING WITHIN THE FAMILY

"In this family, we value having a mentor."

Key Word: Mentor

Start by asking everyone in the family:

"What do you think the word 'Mentor' means?"

Talk about how a mentor is someone who helps guide, teach, and encourage others—not by being perfect, but by leading with kindness and wisdom.

Ask:

- Who has been a mentor in your life?
- What does a good mentor do for others?

Listen to each other's ideas—we'll come back at the end to create our own *Family Definition* of Mentor.

Learn

In a healthy family, everyone can be a mentor to someone else.

Mentors help others grow by:

- Teaching what they know
- Modelling kindness, patience, and responsibility
- Encouraging others to keep learning
- Sharing stories of what they've learned
- Walking alongside someone—not controlling them

Being a mentor happens in little moments—not by giving big speeches, but by living in a way others can follow.

Families grow stronger when older family members guide younger ones—and when everyone is willing to teach and learn from each other.

Consider

Go around the family and talk about:

Tell us about a time when someone mentored you or helped guide you through something new.

Then share:

What is tricky about being a mentor at home?

(E.g., feeling impatient, forgetting to encourage, not setting a good example)

Discuss

Ask these questions and listen well:

- Why is being a mentor important in family life?
- What happens when we forget people are learning from us?
- What could we practise this week to grow as family mentors?

Do

This week, practise being a mentor at home:

- Help younger family members learn new skills.
- Name one person who you can approach and ask to mentor you. What do you notice about their character that you want to learn?
- Encourage each other when someone is trying hard or learning something new.
- Look for moments to teach, guide, and lead by example.

End-of-Week Reflection

Gather as a family and talk about:

- Did we practise being good mentors this week?
- What helped us guide and encourage each other?
- What will we keep doing to stay a family who mentors with kindness and love?

Family Definition

As a family, agree together:

What do we want the word 'Mentor' to mean in our home?

Write your family definition here:

_____

_____

_____

_____

WEEK 33:

MANAGING FAMILY PRIORITIES

"In this family, we focus on what matters most—each other."

Key Word: Focus

Start by asking everyone in the family:

"What do you think the word 'Focus' means?"

Talk about how focus is about paying attention to what matters most—
not getting distracted by everything else.

Ask:

- What helps you focus at home or at school?
- What happens when we lose focus as a family?

Listen to each other's ideas—we'll come back at the end to create our
own *Family Definition* of Focus.

Learn

Every family has lots to do—but not everything is equally important.

Focus helps us:

- Pay attention to the people and moments that matter most
- Finish what we start
- Say no to distractions
- Be present with each other
- Keep our family values at the centre of what we do

Without focus, life gets rushed, busy, and disconnected.

With focus, we slow down, connect deeply, and live with purpose.

Consider

Encourage everyone to share their thoughts:

Tell us about a time when you stayed focused and it helped you or others.

Then share:

What is tricky about staying focused in our family?

(E.g., too many activities, screen time, forgetting what's most important)

Discuss

Explore these questions together as a family:

- Why is focus important in family life?

- What happens when we lose focus on what matters most?
- What could we practise this week to help us stay focused on each other?

Do

Find ways this week to:

- Slow down at family meals—talk and listen well.
- Limit distractions during important times (like family games, meals, or bedtime).
- Make a list of the most important things we want to focus on as a family (e.g., kindness, helping, fun, learning).
- Notice when someone is doing a great job focusing—and encourage them.

End-of-Week Reflection

Gather as a family and talk about:

- Did we practise focus well this week?
- What helped us pay attention to what matters most?
- What will we keep doing to stay a family who lives with focus and purpose?

Family Definition

As a family, agree together:

What do we want the word 'Focus' to mean in our home?

Write your family definition here:

_____

_____

_____

_____

WEEK 34:

FAMILY PROBLEM-SOLVING SKILLS

"In this family, we don't stay stuck—we look for solutions together."

Key Word: Solutions

Start by asking everyone in the family:

"What do you think the word 'Solutions' means?"

Talk about how solutions are the creative ideas and actions we come up with to fix problems or make situations better.

Ask:

- What makes someone a good problem-solver?
- How do we find good solutions together as a family?

Listen to each other's ideas—we'll come back at the end to create our own *Family Definition* of Solutions.

Learn

Every family faces problems—small ones and big ones.

Healthy families don't ignore problems or stay stuck in blame—they work together to find solutions.

Problem-solving in a family means:

- Staying calm
- Listening to everyone's ideas
- Working together—not against each other
- Being creative with options
- Choosing a solution that helps everyone
- Learning from what worked (or didn't)

Solutions come when we focus on what we *can* do—not just what's gone wrong.

Consider

Let everyone have a turn sharing:

Tell us about a time when our family worked together to find a solution to a problem. What happened?

Then share:

What is tricky about solving problems well in our family?

(E.g., interrupting, wanting to win, giving up quickly)

Discuss

Talk about these questions together:

- Why is problem-solving important in family life?
- What happens when people stay focused on the problem instead of looking for solutions?
- What could we practise this week to become better problem-solvers together?

Do

This week, practise finding solutions together at home:

- Pause when a problem comes up.
- Ask: "What's the best solution for everyone here?"
- Use the GROW or Empowerment Model if helpful.
- Celebrate creative or thoughtful solutions people come up with.

End-of-Week Reflection

Gather as a family and talk about:

- Did we practise problem-solving well this week?
- What helped us find creative solutions together?
- What will we keep doing to stay a family who solves problems with kindness and teamwork?

Family Definition

As a family, agree together:

What do we want the word 'Solutions' to mean in our home?

Write your family definition here:

_____

_____

_____

_____

WEEK 35:

EMPOWERING FAMILY CHOICES

*"In this family, freedom means making good
choices and owning them."*

Key Word: Freedom

Start by asking everyone in the family:

"What do you think the word 'Freedom' means?"

Talk about how freedom in a family doesn't mean doing whatever you want. It means having the ability to make good choices and take responsibility for them.

Ask:

- What does healthy freedom look like in our home?
- What happens when people misuse their freedom?

Listen to each other's ideas—we'll come back at the end to create our own *Family Definition* of Freedom.

Learn

Freedom is not the opposite of responsibility—they actually go together.

True freedom happens when we:

- Make wise choices
- Take ownership of our actions
- Respect other people's freedom and boundaries
- Choose love over control

In a healthy family, freedom means:

- You get to make choices
- You are responsible for the outcome
- You learn from mistakes
- You grow stronger and wiser

Without freedom, people feel controlled or stuck.

Without responsibility, freedom becomes selfish or careless.

We want to be a family who practises both freedom *and* responsibility.

Consider

Invite each person to share:

Tell us about a time when you used your freedom to make a really good choice. How did that feel?

Then share:

What is tricky about using freedom well in our family?

(E.g., not thinking about others, forgetting responsibility, acting without care)

Discuss

Use these questions to guide your family conversation:

- Why is freedom important in family life?
- What happens when people forget responsibility with their freedom?
- What could we practise this week to use our freedom in healthy, kind ways?

Do

This week, see what happens when you:

- Look for moments to make good choices without being told.
- Think about how your actions affect others.
- Celebrate when someone uses freedom to make a wise or kind choice.
- Remind each other: "Freedom means I'm responsible for what I choose."

End-of-Week Reflection

Gather as a family and talk about:

- Did we practise healthy freedom well this week?

- What helped us make good choices on our own?

- What will we keep doing to stay a family who uses freedom with kindness and responsibility?

Family Definition

As a family, agree together:

What do we want the word 'Freedom' to mean in our home?

Write your family definition here:

_____

_____

_____

_____

WEEK 36:

HEALTHY BOUNDARIES FOR FAMILY LONGEVITY

"In this family, space is a gift we give to care for ourselves and each other."

Key Word: Space

Start by asking everyone in the family:

"What do you think the word 'Space' means?"

Talk about how space isn't just about physical distance—it's about creating healthy boundaries, giving people time to think, feel, calm down, or recharge.

Ask:

- When do you need space at home?
- How does giving and respecting space help our family stay connected?

Listen to each other's ideas—we'll come back at the end to create our own *Family Definition* of Space.

Learn

Healthy families know that connection grows best when people also have space.

Space helps us:

- Calm down when we feel upset
- Think before we speak or act
- Recharge when we feel tired or overwhelmed
- Show respect for others' feelings, needs, and boundaries

Without space, people can feel pressured, overwhelmed, or crowded.

With space, people feel respected, safe, and ready to connect again.

Giving space doesn't mean we don't care—it shows love, patience, and understanding.

Consider

Ask everyone to share a story or example:

Tell us about a time when having space helped you feel better, calmer, or more ready to connect.

Then share:

What is tricky about giving or asking for space in our family?

(E.g., wanting to fix things straight away, feeling hurt, not knowing how to ask for it kindly)

Discuss

Go around the family and share your thoughts:

- Why is space important in family life?
- What happens when people don't respect someone's need for space?
- What could we practise this week to create healthy space for each other?

Do

Throughout the week, look for ways to:

- Ask for space kindly if you need to calm down or think.
- Respect when someone else asks for space.
- Check in after giving space to reconnect well.
- Remind each other: "Space helps us stay connected."

End-of-Week Reflection

Gather as a family and talk about:

- Did we practise healthy space well this week?
- What helped us give or receive space in loving ways?
- What will we keep doing to stay a family who uses space to protect connection?

Family Definition

As a family, agree together:

What do we want the word 'Space' to mean in our home?

Write your family definition here:

_____

_____

_____

_____

WEEK 37:

CELEBRATING FAMILY SUCCESSES

*"In this family, we celebrate every win—big or small
—because every step forward matters."*

Key Word: Success

Start by asking everyone in the family:

"What do you think the word 'Success' means?"

Talk about how success doesn't always mean winning or being the best—it's about growing, learning, showing kindness, or reaching a goal that matters to you.

Ask:

- What does success look like in everyday family life?
- Can success look different for different people?

Listen to each other's ideas—we'll come back at the end to create our own *Family Definition* of Success.

Learn

Success in family life isn't just about big achievements—it's about celebrating progress, growth, and effort.

Success looks like:

- Trying your best, even when it's hard
- Learning something new
- Being kind in a difficult situation
- Overcoming a fear
- Working together as a team
- Reaching a family goal

Healthy families celebrate not just *what* people achieve, but *who* they are becoming along the way.

Success grows where encouragement and love are present.

Consider

Go around the family and talk about:

Tell us about a time when you felt really successful. What happened and why did it feel good?

Then share:

What is tricky about recognising success in everyday family life?

(E.g., forgetting to notice, comparing to others, only celebrating big moments)

Discuss

Pick one or two questions to start your conversation:

- Why is success important in family life?
- How can we celebrate progress—not just perfection?
- What could we practise this week to recognise success in everyday moments?

Do

This week, practise recognising and celebrating success at home:

- Look for small wins and effort—not just results.
- Celebrate when someone shows kindness, courage, or growth.
- Share "success stories" at dinner or bedtime.
- Remind each other: "Success looks different for everyone—and that's okay."

Create a *Family Success Wall*—write sticky notes, add photos, or draw moments of success from the week.

End-of-Week Reflection

Gather as a family and talk about:

- Did we practise celebrating success well this week?
- What helped us recognise everyday wins and growth?

- What will we keep doing to stay a family who values real success?

Family Definition

As a family, agree together:

What do we want the word 'Success' to mean in our home?

Write your family definition here:

_____

_____

_____

_____

WEEK 38:

ENCOURAGING GROWTH IN EACH FAMILY MEMBER

"In this family, we see the gold in each other and help it grow."

Key Word: Potential

Start by asking everyone in the family:

"What do you think the word 'Potential' means?"

Talk about how potential means the possibility of what you could become—your talents, character, and skills that are still growing and developing.

Ask:

- What does it look like when someone is growing into their potential?
- How do we help each other reach our potential in our family?

Listen to each other's ideas—we'll come back at the end to create our own *Family Definition* of Potential.

Learn

Every person has potential—things inside them that haven't been fully seen or developed yet.

Families help unlock potential when they:

- Speak words of encouragement
- Notice growth, effort, and character
- Support dreams and goals
- Give feedback with love
- Believe in each other even on hard days

When we focus only on mistakes, we shrink back.

When we focus on potential, we move forward.

Encouraging potential helps people feel safe to try, learn, and grow.

Consider

Encourage everyone to share their thoughts:

Tell us about a time when someone believed in your potential. How did that help you grow?

Then share:

What is tricky about encouraging potential in our family?

(E.g., focusing on mistakes, being impatient, wanting quick results)

Discuss

Take turns answering these:

- Why is encouraging potential important in family life?
- What happens when people feel like no one sees their growth?
- What could we practise this week to help each other grow into our potential?

Do

Challenge yourself this week to:

- Speak words of belief and encouragement.
- Notice and celebrate growth—not just achievements.
- Ask each person: "What's something you're working on growing in?"
- Remind each other: "You have so much potential. I believe in you."

End-of-Week Reflection

Gather as a family and talk about:

- Did we practise encouraging potential well this week?
- What helped us see and celebrate each other's growth?
- What will we keep doing to stay a family who believes in each other's potential?

Family Definition

As a family, agree together:

What do we want the word 'Potential' to mean in our home?

Write your family definition here:

_____

_____

_____

_____

WEEK 39:

HANDLING DISAPPOINTMENT TOGETHER

"In this family, we feel big feelings—but we stay strong and keep going."

Key Word: Emotional Strength

Start by asking everyone in the family:

"What do you think the words 'Emotional Strength' mean?"

Talk about how emotional strength is not about never feeling sad or upset—it's about learning to handle big feelings well, bounce back from disappointment, and stay connected to others.

Ask:

- What does emotional strength look like in everyday life?
- How do we build emotional strength as a family?

Listen to each other's ideas—we'll come back at the end to create our own *Family Definition* of Emotional Strength.

Learn

Life won't always go our way—and that's okay.

Emotional strength helps us:

- Feel our feelings fully without shame
- Talk about what's going on inside us
- Take a break when needed
- Learn and grow from disappointment
- Keep going when things feel hard

In strong families, people feel safe to express their feelings—but they also practise calming down, learning from the moment, and moving forward with courage.

Emotional strength is like a muscle—the more we use it, the stronger it gets.

Consider

Let everyone have a turn sharing:

Tell us about a time when you showed emotional strength. How did you handle a hard or disappointing moment?

Then share:

What is tricky about showing emotional strength in our family?

(E.g., feeling stuck in sadness or frustration, reacting quickly, not knowing what to say)

Discuss

Choose a few of these questions as a family:

- Why is emotional strength important in family life?
- What happens when we don't handle disappointment well?
- What could we practise this week to build emotional strength together?

Do

This week, notice how it feels when you:

- Talk about your feelings honestly.
- Take a moment to breathe and calm down before reacting.
- Encourage each other in hard moments.
- Look for what you can learn or how you can grow from disappointment.

End-of-Week Reflection

Gather as a family and talk about:

- Did we practise emotional strength well this week?
- What helped us handle disappointment in healthy ways?
- What will we keep doing to stay a family who builds emotional strength together?

Family Definition

As a family, agree together:

What do we want the words 'Emotional Strength' to mean in our home?

Write your family definition here:

_____

_____

_____

_____

WEEK 40:

CELEBRATING FAMILY AND PERSONAL GROWTH

"In this family, we celebrate progress—not perfection."

Key Word: Celebrate

Start by asking everyone in the family:

"What do you think the word 'Celebrate' means?"

Talk about how celebrating means stopping to notice and enjoy the good things—big or small—especially the ways we've grown and loved each other well.

Ask:

- What do we love celebrating together?
- Why is it important to celebrate growth—not just achievements?

We'll come back at the end to create our own *Family Definition* of Celebrate.

Learn

Healthy families pause to celebrate progress—not just perfection.

This year, we've grown together in four big areas:

- Building Healthy Relationships
- Practising Joyful Responsibility
- Living out Genuine Restoration
- Creating a Culture of Love

Celebrating reminds us of how far we've come—and gives us courage to keep growing.

Consider

As a family, go through the four key areas and score each one out of 10.

(1 = we really struggled this year, 10 = we've grown so much here)

Healthy Relationships (/10)

Joyful Responsibility (/10)

Genuine Restoration (/10)

Culture of Love (/10)

Talk about why you gave that score—and what you are most proud of in that area.

Then share:

- What have we grown in the most this year?
- What was the hardest thing for us to practise?
- What helped us stay connected and strong as a family?

Discuss

Let everyone have a turn sharing:

- What was your favourite thing we learned together this year?
- What changed about how our family feels and acts now?
- What do we want to keep practising to keep growing and loving well?

Do

Do this together as a family:

- Encourage each person—tell them what you've seen grow in them.
- Share favourite family memories or funny moments from the year.
- Decide on one thing you want to keep growing in for the next year.
- Celebrate together—have a meal, a treat, a game night, or something fun that marks this special moment.

End-of-Week Reflection

Gather as a family and talk about:

- What helped us grow the most this year?
- What are we most proud of as a family?
- What will we keep doing to stay a family who loves, grows, and celebrates together?

Family Definition

As a family, agree together:

What do we want the word 'Celebrate' to mean in our home?

Write your family definition here:

_____

_____

_____

_____

BONUS TOPICS

Think of this Bonus Section as some extra goodness for those weeks when the term runs a little longer than usual!

These extra sessions are designed to build on everything your family has already learned—giving you more chances to reflect, grow, and keep building their leadership muscles. Whether it's diving deeper into responsibility, strengthening relationships, or growing in personal confidence, these sessions offer fresh challenges and meaningful conversations to keep the momentum going.

It's all about continuing the journey and giving you more space to grow into the powerful, respectful, and connected people and family you're becoming.

BONUS TOPIC 1:

CHOICES AND CONSEQUENCES IN THE FAMILY

"In this family, we understand that every choice brings a consequence—and we learn from both."

Key Word: Consequence

Start by asking everyone in the family:

"What do you think the word 'Consequence' means?"

Talk about how a consequence is what happens after we make a choice—sometimes good, sometimes challenging, but always connected to what we chose.

Ask:

- What are some examples of good consequences?
- What are some examples of tricky consequences?

We'll come back at the end to create our own *Family Definition* of Consequence.

Learn

Every choice leads somewhere.

In a family, we want to remember that consequences are not about punishment—they are about learning and growing.

Healthy families help each other understand:

- Our choices create outcomes
- Good choices lead to good consequences
- Poor choices lead to learning moments
- Taking responsibility for consequences helps us grow stronger

Knowing that consequences follow choices helps us think ahead and make decisions that build trust, connection, and respect.

Consider

Invite each person to share:

Tell us about a time when you made a great choice. What was the positive consequence?

Then share:

Tell us about a time when you made a poor choice. What did you learn from the consequence?

Discuss

Choose a few of these questions as a family:

- Why are consequences important in family life?
- What happens when people avoid taking responsibility for consequences?
- What could we practise this week to grow in understanding consequences together?

Do

See what happens when you:

- Notice when a good consequence happens—celebrate it.
- Talk kindly and clearly when a poor choice leads to a hard consequence.
- Encourage each other to take responsibility and learn from every experience.
- Use the phrase: "Choices bring consequences—and we get to learn from them."

End-of-Week Reflection

Gather as a family and talk about:

- What good consequences did we notice this week?
- What helped us learn from poor choices or tricky consequences?
- What will we keep doing to stay a family who learns and grows from consequences?

Family Definition

As a family, agree together:

What do we want the word 'Consequence' to mean in our home?

Write your family definition here:

_____

_____

_____

_____

BONUS TOPIC 2:

SETTING FAMILY AND PERSONAL GOALS

*"In this family, we grow on purpose—we set goals
and go after them together."*

Key Word: Goals

Start by asking everyone in the family:

"What do you think the word 'Goals' means?"

Talk about how goals are things we work towards—something we want to learn, improve, or achieve together.

Ask:

- Why are goals helpful in a family?
- What happens when we don't have clear goals?

We'll come back at the end to create our own *Family Definition* of Goals.

Learn

In our family, we use the GROW Problem-Solving Model to help us set and reach goals.

G—Goal: What do we want to happen?

R—Roadblocks: What's getting in the way?

O—Options: What are all the ideas we can think of to help?

W—Way Forward: What is our plan—and what will we do next?

Goals help us focus on what matters most. They give us direction and something to work towards as a family.

Consider

Go around the family and answer:

Tell us about a goal you have worked towards—what helped you reach it?

Then share:

What is tricky about setting goals or following through in our family?

Discuss

As a family, use the GROW Steps to set some family goals for this season.

Examples could include:

- Spending more time together
- Being more helpful without being asked
- Speaking kindly and listening better
- Learning or trying something new as a family

Do

Write down 2–3 family goals together that you would like to work on.

Family Goals:

1. _____
2. _____
3. _____

Now, give each person a chance to write down 3 personal goals—things they want to grow in or work on.

Personal Goals:

1. _____
2. _____
3. _____

Talk about:

- Why these goals matter to us
- What will help us stay focused
- How we want to celebrate progress

This week, practise encouraging each other and taking steps towards your goals.

End-of-Week Reflection

Gather as a family and talk about:

- What goals did we set this week?
- What helped us take action?
- What will we keep doing to stay a family who grows, learns, and sets goals together?

Family Definition

As a family, agree together:

What do we want the word 'Goals' to mean in our home?

Write your family definition here:

_____

_____

_____

_____

BONUS TOPIC 3:

INCLUSION AND DIVERSITY AT HOME

"In this family, everyone belongs just as they are."

Key Word: Inclusion

Start by asking everyone in the family:

"What do you think the word 'Inclusion' means?"

Talk about how inclusion means making sure everyone feels welcome, valued, and accepted—especially those who are different from us.

Ask:

- What helps people feel included at home, at school, or in a group?
- What happens when someone feels left out or unseen?

We'll come back at the end to create our own *Family Definition* of Inclusion.

Learn

Healthy families practise inclusion.

Inclusion is not about everyone being the same—it's about making space for each person's uniqueness.

Inclusion means:

- Everyone belongs
- Everyone is seen and heard
- Everyone is respected
- Everyone has something valuable to bring

Inclusion celebrates that we are all different—and that diversity makes life richer and more interesting.

Consider

Ask everyone to share a story or example:

Tell us about a time when you felt included. What did someone do that helped you feel welcome?

Then share:

What is tricky about practising inclusion in our family?

(E.g., forgetting to include younger siblings, only playing with certain people, not noticing who feels left out)

Discuss

Use these questions to explore the idea of Diversity together:

- What makes each person in our family different or unique?

- Why is it important to have people in our lives who think, look, or act differently to us?

- What happens when families or groups only include people who are the same?

- What could we practise this week to include and celebrate diversity better?

Do

Challenge yourself this week to:

- Look for people (even outside your family) who might feel left out.

- Invite them to join in, sit with you, or be part of what you're doing.

- Practise including everyone in family activities.

- Celebrate differences—talk about what makes each family member special.

End-of-Week Reflection

Gather as a family and talk about:

- What helped us practise inclusion well this week?

- What did we learn about diversity and celebrating differences?

- What will we keep doing to stay a family who values inclusion?

Family Definition

As a family, agree together:

What do we want the word 'Inclusion' to mean in our home?

Write your family definition here:

_____

_____

_____

_____

BONUS TOPIC 4:

NAVIGATING PEER PRESSURE AS A FAMILY

"In this family, we lead ourselves with courage—even if no one else is."

Key Word: Peer Pressure

Start by asking everyone in the family:

"What do you think the words 'Peer Pressure' mean?"

Talk about how peer pressure is when people around us try to influence our choices—sometimes in positive ways, sometimes in unhelpful ways.

Ask:

- When do people feel peer pressure?
- What helps someone stay true to themselves in those moments?

We'll come back at the end to create our own *Family Definition* of Peer Pressure.

Learn

Everyone faces peer pressure—especially at school, in friendships, or online.

Peer pressure can sound like:

- "Everyone else is doing it."
- "If you don't do this, you won't fit in."
- "Don't be boring."
- "Nobody will find out."

But in our family, we want to remember:

- We always have a choice.
- We are powerful people who lead ourselves first.
- We don't have to copy what others do—especially if it's unkind, unsafe, or goes against our values.

Healthy families talk about peer pressure openly, and practise standing strong together.

Consider

Encourage everyone to share their thoughts:

Tell us about a time when you felt peer pressure. What did you do, and how did it feel?

Then share:

What helps us handle peer pressure well?

(E.g., knowing your values, having a plan, saying no kindly)

Discuss

Let everyone have a turn sharing:

- Why is peer pressure hard sometimes?
- What happens when we follow others instead of leading our-selves?
- What could we practise this week to stay true to who we want to be—even when it's hard?

Talk about:

- How can we encourage each other to make good choices?
- What does our family want to be known for?

Do

This week, practise noticing peer pressure moments—and talk about them together.

Encourage each other to:

- Think before acting.
- Ask: "Is this who I want to be?"
- Speak kindly but clearly if saying no.
- Remember: "I get to choose my actions—no one chooses for me."

End-of-Week Reflection

Gather as a family and talk about:

- What peer pressure moments did we notice this week?
- What helped us stay strong and make good choices?
- What will we keep doing to stay a family who leads themselves well?

Family Definition

As a family, agree together:

What do we want the words 'Peer Pressure' to mean in our home?

Write your family definition here:

_____

_____

_____

_____

HOLIDAY TOPICS

Strong Families Keep Growing—Even on Holidays

School holidays and family downtime are a special opportunity to slow down, reconnect, and have fun together.

But just because routines change, it doesn't mean we stop building our family culture of love, connection, responsibility, and restoration.

These Holiday Topics are designed to keep the heart of your family growing in fun, active, and creative ways.

They are simple.

They are playful.

And they're a great way to practise everything you've been learning together all year.

Each topic will give you a short, practical activity or challenge, plus a few questions to help keep conversation flowing naturally.

You don't have to do them in order.

You don't need anything fancy to get started.

Just choose a topic when it suits you and enjoy the moments of laughter, connection, teamwork, and growth that will naturally happen along the way.

Four Themes--Sixteen Topics

We've grouped the holiday topics around the four key areas that help create strong families:

- Healthy Relationships
- Joyful Responsibility
- Genuine Restoration
- A Culture of Love

Use them at home, on holidays, in the car, at mealtimes, or even on the go.

Strong families don't happen by accident—they grow one small moment at a time.

Enjoy making memories together and keep building your culture of love in every season.

HEALTHY RELATIONSHIPS
—HOLIDAY TOPICS

1. Kind Words Challenge

Set a timer for 5 minutes. Go around the family and say as many kind words or compliments as you can to each other.

Talk about:

- How did that feel?
- What happens in a family when kind words become normal?

_____

_____

_____

_____

2. Connection Adventure

Plan a family activity where everyone stays off devices for an hour.

Go for a walk, have a picnic, play a game—just connect.

Talk about:

- What helped us feel connected?
- How do we protect connection in busy life?

_____

_____

_____

_____

3. Listening Tag

Play a game where you can only tag someone after listening to them answer a question.

Talk about:

- Why is listening important in relationships?
- What helps us listen well at home?

_____

_____

_____

_____

4. Family Appreciation Game

Write everyone's name on a piece of paper. Pass it around and write one thing you appreciate about that person.

Read them out loud and celebrate.

_____

_____

_____

_____

Create your own family activity and record it here:

JOYFUL RESPONSIBILITY —HOLIDAY TOPICS

5. Surprise Helper Game

Pick a name secretly. Do something helpful for that person without telling them.

Reveal at the end of the day who your person was!

Talk about:

- How does it feel when people take responsibility for helping?

_____

_____

_____

_____

6. Creative Chore Challenge

Set a timer and see how fast (and well) you can work together to clean or organise a space.

Make it fun—play music or have a silly prize.

_____

_____

_____

_____

7. Kindness Scavenger Hunt

Create a list of small acts of kindness to do during the day (e.g., make someone a drink, offer help, write a note).

Celebrate when all are completed!

_____

_____

_____

_____

8. Ownership Bingo

Create a simple bingo sheet with ideas like:

- Finish a job without being asked
- Clean your space
- Help a family member
- Say sorry quickly

See who can get bingo first.

_____

_____

_____

_____

Create your own family activity and record it here:

GENUINE RESTORATION —HOLIDAY TOPICS

9. Role Play Apologies

Take turns acting out silly scenarios where someone needs to say sorry.

Practise:

- Owning the mistake
- Saying sorry well
- Asking to make it right

_____

_____

_____

_____

10. Family Repair Walk

Go for a walk together and talk about:

- Is there anything we need to clear up or talk about?

- What helps us restore connection after a disagreement?

_____

_____

_____

_____

11. Second Chances Storytime

Each person shares a story of when they needed a second chance—or gave one.

Celebrate the beauty of grace.

_____

_____

_____

_____

12. Restoration Relay

Set up a fun obstacle course or relay where the goal is not to win—but to help each other finish well.

Talk about:

- How do we help each other restore and finish strong?

_____

_____

_____

_____

Create your own family activity and record it here:

A CULTURE OF LOVE
—HOLIDAY TOPICS

13. Love in Action Day

As a family, pick one person outside your home to show love to today.

Ideas could include:

- Baking for a neighbour
- Sending an encouraging message
- Helping someone in need

_____

_____

_____

_____

Talk about:

- How does love become real when we show it in action?

_____

_____

_____

_____

14. Family Gratitude Hunt

Spend 10 minutes finding things around the house you're thankful for—people, objects, memories.

Share them together and talk about:

- How does gratitude help create a culture of love?

_____

_____

_____

_____

15. Celebration Circle

Sit in a circle. Take turns saying:

- "One thing I love about our family is…"

Keep going until everyone has shared multiple things.

Talk about:

- How does celebrating the good protect our connection?

_____

_____

_____

_____

16. Secret Encourager

Assign each family member a secret "encourager" role for the day.

Leave notes, do acts of kindness, or look for ways to build them up.

Reveal your encourager at the end of the day.

Talk about:

- What changes when our home is full of encouragement?

_____

_____

_____

_____

Create your own family activity and record it here:

YOUR FAMILY MANIFESTO

This is your moment to capture who you are becoming as a family. Over the past year, you've taken time each week to practise connection, responsibility, restoration, and love.

You've created Family Phrases, written Family Definitions, shared stories, solved problems, forgiven mistakes, and celebrated growth.

Now it's time to put it all together and write your Family Manifesto—a few sentences that capture who you want to be as a family moving forward.

This isn't about getting it perfect—it's about writing words that remind you of what matters most in your home.

Make it simple or make it creative—just make it yours.

Use these prompts to guide your Family Manifesto discussion and take notes of key words, ideas, or phrases.

In this family, we…

What do we want to be known for?

_____

_____

_____

_____

We choose to…

What actions or attitudes matter most in our home?

_____

_____

_____

_____

We believe that…

What values do we want to live by?

_____

_____

_____

_____

The words that describe our family best are…

What words would you hope others see in your family culture?

_____

_____

_____

_____

We are a Culture of… (choose one word)

_____

_____

_____

_____

Write Your Family Manifesto

Once you've written your Family Manifesto, you might like to:

- Display it somewhere special in your home—you might choose to frame it, design it creatively, or make it a feature in your family space.
- Add drawings, signatures, or handprints from each family member.
- Read it together regularly—especially when challenges arise.
- Revisit it each year and add to it as your family grows and changes.

This is your family story, your words, your culture.

Be proud of the journey you've taken together.

Example of a Family Manifesto

In this family, we choose love over fear.

We choose kindness, respect, and honesty even when it's hard.

We believe that every person belongs and every voice matters.

We show up for each other, forgive quickly, laugh often, and never give up.

We want to be known for creating a home where people feel safe, seen, and loved.

The words that describe our family best are: love, courage, fun, kindness, and connection.

We are a Culture of Love.

Write Your Family Manifesto Here

The Culture Momentum Pocketbook Series

OUR FAMILY CULTURE STATEMENTS

In this family, we listen with our hearts—because every voice matters.

In this family, we give and receive feedback with honesty, kindness, and care.

In this family, we care about how others feel—and we try to understand before we respond.

In this family, we speak love in a way others can understand.

In this family, we solve problems together—with courage, calm, and care.

In this family, we show respect to ourselves and others.

In this family, we're better together—we look out for one another and work as a team.

In this family, we build trust by doing what's right—even when it's hard.

In this family, we take responsibility for our choices and how we treat each other.

In this family, we choose friendships that lift others up and help us grow.

In this family, we use our freedom to make powerful choices.

In this family, we take responsibility for our part—even when it's hard.

In this family, we use love as our guide—not fear, control, or shame.

In this family, we learn how to speak each other's love languages.

In this family, we honour ourselves and others by setting healthy boundaries.

In this family, we take ownership of our own actions—and let others take ownership of theirs.

In this family, we make space to learn from our mistakes and try again.

In this family, we encourage each other to grow.

In this family, we practise what we say matters—not just when it's easy, but when it counts.

In this family, we show responsibility through our words, our attitude, and our actions.

In this family, we say sorry when we've hurt someone—and we mean it.

In this family, we forgive—not to excuse what happened, but to heal and move forward.

In this family, we rebuild trust by choosing truth, kindness, and consistency.

In this family, we believe in second chances—because everyone is growing.

In this family, we own our behaviour—even when things go wrong.

In this family, we build strong friendships that bring out the best in us.

In this family, we take responsibility for ourselves—and lead others with kindness.

In this family, we treat ourselves with the same respect we show others.

In this family, we do something when we see a problem—even if we didn't cause it.

In this family, we lead by example—with love, respect, and consistency.

In this family, leadership is about how we live, not just what we say.

In this family, we use our words to lift others up—and cheer each other on.

In this family, we focus on what matters—not just what's urgent.

In this family, we face challenges together—with honesty, hope, and strength.

In this family, we support each other—but we don't take over.

In this family, we protect what matters most—our peace, our purpose, and our people.

In this family, we celebrate the wins, the growth, and the moments that matter.

In this family, we lift others—we don't just lead them.

In this family, we choose to keep going—even when we feel disappointed.

In this family, we stop to notice how far we've come—and celebrate the journey.

In this family, we take responsibility for our choices—because freedom and accountability go hand in hand.

In this family, we grow on purpose—not by pressure, but with clarity and direction.

In this family, everyone belongs—not by being the same, but by being truly seen and valued.

In this family, we choose integrity over approval—and lead with courage, not conformity.

A FINAL NOTE FROM ME TO YOU

Dear Family,

Thank you for taking this journey. Thank you for showing up—not perfectly, but on purpose. Thank you for creating space in the middle of busy family life to have conversations that matter. For listening to each other. For laughing together. For working through the messy moments. For trying again.

This resource was never about getting everything right. It's about building something real. A family culture where connection isn't accidental—it's intentional. Where love isn't just a feeling—it's a practice. Where responsibility isn't heavy—it's joyful. Where mistakes aren't final—they're part of the learning.

If you've made it this far, you are already that family. Not perfect. Not finished. But becoming.

My hope is that this year has given you shared language, memorable moments, and a deeper sense of who you are becoming together. I pray your Family Room is filled with reminders of love, courage, responsibility, forgiveness, and growth—but more than that, I pray those words are written on your hearts, lived out in the ordinary, unseen moments of everyday life.

Keep Choosing Connection,

Bernii Godwin

EQUIPPING A CULTURE OF LOVE

At Godwin Consulting, we believe in empowering families, educators, and leaders to create environments where joy, responsibility, and connection thrive. That's why we've designed a variety of resources to support you on your journey—whether you're nurturing your family at home, supporting students in classrooms, or empowering leaders in your organization.

As you move through this Family Room Edition, we encourage you to think beyond your home environment. Many parents are also leaders in workplaces, schools, or community settings. The same culture of love, responsibility, and restoration you are cultivating in your family can also transform the teams you lead.

If you lead staff or teams at work, consider walking them through a similar culture journey using our LoSoP Culture: Boardroom or Staffroom Editions. This resource has been specifically designed to help leaders build connected, respectful, and empowered workplace cultures. It follows the same principles and weekly topics as the Family Room Edition, but with a leadership and team focus.

Alongside this, we offer a variety of tools to equip you further:

- Practical family tools like our LoSoP Desk Flip and Language Flashcards
- The empowering Umbrella of Grace for daily reminders of compassion
- Printable posters to keep the LoSoP philosophy front and centre
- Online courses for parents, educators, and leaders exploring the neuroscience of connection and LoSoP principles
- The LoSoP Foundations Course for deeper exploration into Loving our Students on Purpose.

Visit our online store at **www.godwinconsulting.com.au** to explore all of these resources. We're here to support you in nurturing stronger, more connected communities—both at home and at work.

Building a culture of love doesn't happen overnight, but with small, consistent steps in both family and workplace settings, you can create environments where people feel safe, valued, and deeply connected.

ABOUT THE AUTHOR

Bernii Godwin holds a Master's qualification in Social Work and a Graduate Certificate in Neuropsychotherapy, building on her undergraduate degree in Human Services and Criminology and Criminal Justice, with a focus on youth and family justice. She is also a certified Loving on Purpose Trainer and John Maxwell Leadership Team Member.

Bernii is the Co-Author of *Loving Our Students On Purpose* with Danny Silk and the creator of the *LoSoP Momentum Series*—a suite of resources designed to support schools, leaders, and families to build cultures of love, responsibility, and connection across all areas of school and family life.

Over the past two decades, Bernii has worked in various roles across a wide range of schools, specialising in student wellbeing and behaviour. Principals frequently seek her expertise to consult on complex behaviour and wellbeing issues, provide one-on-one coaching or supervision to educators and wellbeing teams, and deliver school-wide professional development.

Her greatest passion is helping schools and families adopt practical tools that replace fear and punishment with purposeful behaviour education, safe connection, and empowered leadership—ultimately increasing student engagement and creating environments where people can thrive.

To connect with Bernii, please visit

www.godwinconsulting.com.au

www.ingramcontent.com/pod-product-compliance
Lightning Source LLC
Chambersburg PA
CBHW071938260326
41914CB00004B/668